# UNION-MANAGEMENT COOPERATION

## Structure • Process •Impact

Michael H. Schuster

*Syracuse University*

1984

The W. E. Upjohn Institute for Employment Research

**Library of Congress Cataloging in Publication Data**

Schuster, Michael H.
  Union-management cooperation.

  Includes bibliographical references.

  1. Labor-management committees—United States.
  2. Industrial relations—United States.  I.Title.
  HD6490.L33S38  1984      331'.01'12      84-17373
  ISBN 0-88099-023-6
  ISBN 0-88099-024-4 (pbk.)

# THE AUTHOR

Michael Schuster is associate professor of Personnel and Industrial Relations and director of the Employment Studies Institute at Syracuse University. He has served as a consultant on human resource planning, union-management cooperation, and productivity-gainsharing to various business, labor and government agencies.

Dr. Schuster has published widely in the areas of cooperation and change in union and nonunion environments, quality of worklife, productivity, and employment discrimination. He is co-author of *The Aging Worker: Research and Recommendations* (1983). His published articles have appeared in journals such as *Industrial and Labor Relations Review, Journal of Applied Behavior Science, Human Resource Management,* and *Aging and Work.*

Dr. Schuster holds a B.A. in political science from the University of Rhode Island and an M.S. from the University of Massachusetts Labor Relations and Research Center. He received his J.D. and Ph.D. from Syracuse University.

This book is dedicated to my grandparents —

Michael and Annie Harrison

and

Isadore and Clara Schuster

# FOREWORD

Although cooperative union-management programs are not new to the American scene, their increasingly widespread use during the past decade suggests a need for systematic study and evaluation of these efforts and their outcomes. This study by Schuster demonstrates the application of a theory-based approach to the examination of such programs.

Using a combination of empirical and case study procedures, the author examines the structure of six different forms of cooperative experiments, analyzes their implementation process, and assesses their impact. His findings identify a number of factors and conditions associated with successful cooperation and document a significant potential for improvement in company performance and overall labor-management relations. The study is unique because of (1) its large sample size; (2) its use of actual performance measures to assess program outcomes; and (3) its longitudinal design to measure impacts over time.

Facts and observations expressed in this study are the sole responsibility of the author. His viewpoints do not necessarily represent positions of the W. E. Upjohn Institute for Employment Research.

Robert G. Spiegelman
*Director*

*September 1984*

vi

# PREFACE

I first became interested in studying union-management cooperation after reading James Healy's book, *Creative Collective Bargaining*. A model of organizational change in the context of union-management relations developed by Thomas Kochan and Lee Dyer (1976) fortified my interest in the subject matter and stimulated me to further pursue this area of inquiry. The project began in November 1977 as my doctoral dissertation. I am very grateful to Professors Donald DeSalvia, R.J. Chesser, and Susan Rhodes for their support, encouragement, and ideas in the initial phases of this project.

In addition to the sponsorship provided by the W.E. Upjohn Institute for Employment Research, earlier portions of the research were supported by grants from the United States Department of Labor (Grant No. 91-36-79-10) and the National Science Foundation (DAR 80-11866). I am very grateful to the funding organizations for their support. As always, the views expressed in this book do not necessarily represent the official opinion or policy of these agencies. I am solely responsible for the content of this book.

The book attempts to meet the needs of a diverse audience. I hope that students, practitioners, policymakers, and academicians in personnel and industrial relations will find this book beneficial. In many respects, the book may also be appealing to individuals interested in organizational change, since very few studies in this area have examined change and cooperation in unionized plants. Although cooperative union-management programs are not new to the American scene, their increasingly widespread use requires that they be more systematically studied. Hopefully, the findings of this research will influence the practice of industrial relations and future studies of cooperative strategies.

In a large scale research project, the dedicated contributions of a host of individuals are required. Christopher Miller conducted many of the site visits, assisted in the data analysis, drafted portions of chapters, and competently handled numerous tasks related to the management of the project. I am indebted to him for his loyalty to this effort. Robert Ahern, executive director of the Buffalo-Erie County Labor-Management Council, provided the wise guidance of an experienced practitioner of cooperative strategies, as well as assisting in the acquisition of three research sites and commenting on two chapters of the book. I am grateful to Professor Richard McCleary for his willingness to answer my questions on time-series analysis and to Heather Tully for her efforts in keeping the many data sets in good and logical order.

Mary Jo Chase typed endless letters to the research sites requesting an additional data set or data in a different form. Her interest and dedication in her work are most noteworthy. Cindy Clark typed the manuscript and its many revisions.

Most important, this project would not have been possible without the cooperation and patience of union and company personnel at the 38 research sites studied. Their candor in responding to our numerous questions and their willingness to provide as much information as possible has been the key element in the success of this project. Because each research site was guaranteed complete confidentiality, I can only extend an anonymous "thank you" to each person who took time from his/her busy schedule to assist us. Finally, no project of this size could be undertaken without the support and encouragement of one's family. Their understanding on the many occasions when travel took me away from home made the conduct of this project much easier.

Michael H. Schuster
*November 1983*

# CONTENTS

Chapter 1   Introduction ................................... 1
            Importance of Union-Management Cooperation . .   3
            Union and Management Attitudes
                Toward Cooperation ...................... 8
            Structure of the Book ....................... 13

Chapter 2   Models of Change and Cooperation
            in Unionized Settings ........................... 17
            Models of Change and Cooperation ............ 18
                Lawler-Drexler Model .................... 19
                Kochan-Dyer Model ....................... 22
                Nadler, Hanlon, and Lawler Model .......... 25
            Goodman's Model of Scanlon
                Plan Effectiveness....................... 27
            Research Objectives ......................... 28
            Program Structure Research Issues............ 29
            Cooperative Process Research Issues .......... 29
            A Model of Labor-Management
                Productivity Program Effectiveness ........ 31
            Research Hypotheses ...................... 35

Chapter 3   A Research Design for Evaluating
            Cooperative Union-Management Programs .......... 47
            Research Design ........................... 48
                Qualitative Data ......................... 49
                Time-Series Designs ...................... 50
                Sources of Invalidity in Time-Series Designs .... 51
            The Research Sites........................... 53
                Site Selection ........................... 53
                Description of the Research Sites ............ 54
                Control/Comparison Group ................ 58
            Research Strategy .......................... 61
            Methods of Measurement......................62
                Demographic Variables ................... 62
                Study Variable: Productivity ............... 62
                Study Variable: Employment................ 64
                Study Variable: Quality ................... 64
                Study Variables: Unexcused Absenteeism,
                    Voluntary Turnover, Tardiness,
                    and Grievances ...................... 64

Study Variable: Employment Security . . . . . . . . .   65
Study Variable: Employee Participation . . . . . . .   65
Study Variables: Compensation Measures . . . . . .   65
Study Variable: Acceptance Strategy . . . . . . . . . .   66
Additional Study Variables . . . . . . . . . . . . . . . .   66
Methods of Analysis . . . . . . . . . . . . . . . . . . . . . .   67
Productivity, Employment,
and Organizational Effectiveness . . . . . . . . . . .   67
Analysis of Other Study Variables . . . . . . . . . . .   68
Methodological Findings . . . . . . . . . . . . . . . . . . .   69
Finding: The Case Study
Approach Will Continue . . . . . . . . . . . . . . . . .   69
Finding: Industrial Relations Researchers
Can Learn from the Program Evaluators . . . . .   70
Finding: There is a Need
for Longitudinal Studies. . . . . . . . . . . . . . . . . .   70
Finding: Studies Should Utilize
Performance Measures . . . . . . . . . . . . . . . . . . .   71
Finding: Studies Require
Pre-Cooperation Measurement . . . . . . . . . . . .   72
Finding: There is a Need for
Control Group Research . . . . . . . . . . . . . . . . .   72
Finding: There is Difficulty in Obtaining
the Parties' Cooperation . . . . . . . . . . . . . . . . .   72
Finding: The Values of the Investigator
Must be Recognized . . . . . . . . . . . . . . . . . . . .   73
Finding: There is a Need
to Study Unsuccessful Cases . . . . . . . . . . . . . .   73

Chapter 4   A Comparative Analysis of the Structure
of Cooperative Union-Management Interventions . . . . .   75
Degining the Interventions . . . . . . . . . . . . . . . . . .   78
Philosophy/Theory of the Interventions . . . . . . . .   79
Primary Goals of the Program . . . . . . . . . . . . . . .   83
Subsidiary Goals of the Program . . . . . . . . . . . . .   83
Structure for Worker Participation and
Mechanism for Suggestion-Making . . . . . . . . . .   84
Scanlon Plans . . . . . . . . . . . . . . . . . . . . . . . . . . .   84
Quality Circles . . . . . . . . . . . . . . . . . . . . . . . . . . .   85
Rucker Plans . . . . . . . . . . . . . . . . . . . . . . . . . . . .   88
Improshare Plans . . . . . . . . . . . . . . . . . . . . . . . . .   88
Labor-Management Committees. . . . . . . . . . . . . .   89
Quality of Worklife Projects . . . . . . . . . . . . . . . .   91

Impact of An Existing Individual
Suggestion Plan.......................... 91
The Role of Supervision ...................... 92
The Role of Middle and Higher Management ..... 95
Calculation of the Bonus ................... 95
Program Coordinator/Facilitator............ 95
Committee Membership.................... 96
Evaluation of Ideas....................... 96
Productivity-Sharing Formulas ............... 97
The Scanlon Bonus Formula ............... 98
The Rucker Bonus Formula ................ 99
The Improshare Bonus Formula ............ 101
Produced or Shipped Dollars/Hours ......... 103
Benefits from the Bonus Program............ 105
Bonus Formula Manipulation ............... 106
Frequency of Payout....................... 107
Role of the Union .......................... 107
Impact on Management Style ................. 108
Conclusions ............................... 109

Chapter 5   The Process of Change and Cooperation
in Unionized Settings ........................... 111
Introduction............................... 111
The Stimulus for Change .................... 112
The Process of Change ...................... 115
Operational Issues.......................... 118
Perception of the Impact of Change ........... 122
Conclusions ............................... 127

Chapter 6   The Impact of Union-Management Cooperation ...... 129
Summary of Performance Changes ............. 129
Impact Assessments ...................... 129
Determinants of the Effectiveness
of Cooperative Union-Management
Programs ............................. 133
Case Studies of Cooperation ................. 140
Case Study 1: Cooperation
to Save the Plant ....................... 141
Case Study 2: Cooperation to Motivate
the Workforce and Improve the
Quality of Worklife...................... 144
Case Study 3: Evidence of a Delayed Effect..... 150

Case Study 4: The Successful Use
 of a Labor-Management Committee......... 157
Case Study 5: Three Cases of
 Long Term Success ...................... 164
Case Study 6: The Failure to Maintain Equity ... 176
Case Study 7: A Failure to Match the
 Labor-Management Relationship
 With the Intervention .................... 182
Case Study 8: The Failure
 of Cooperation to Take Hold .............. 185
Case Study 9: Mixing QWL Concepts with
 Traditional Union-Management Issues ...... 194
Case Study 10: The Misuse
 of Gainsharing.......................... 202
Conclusions ............................. 212

Chapter 7   Conclusions .................................. 217
The Structure of Cooperation ................. 217
The Process of Cooperation................... 218
The Impact of Cooperation ................... 220
Methodological Findings ..................... 221
Future Research Issues
 Investigation of Additional Research Sites...... 223
Continued Analysis of Selected Sites
 Including Those Where Cooperation
 has Ended............................. 223
Study of Additional Forms
 of Union-Management Cooperation......... 224
Study of Worker-Management
 Cooperation in Nonunion Firms ........... 224
Addition of Attitudinal Variables ............. 224
Analysis of the Calculation of Bonus
 Formulas in Gainsharing Plans ............. 225
Improving the Research Design
 and Analytical Techniques ................ 225

References............................................. 227

# LIST OF TABLES

1-1  Union Attitudes Toward Cooperation . . . . . . . . . . . . . . . . . . . .  9
1-2  Management Attitudes Toward Cooperation . . . . . . . . . . . . . .  14
2-1  Summary of Factors Working For and Against Joint
     Union-Management QWL Projects . . . . . . . . . . . . . . . . . . . .  20
2-2  Summary of the Kochan-Dyer Model of Organizational
     Change in the Context of Union-Management Relations . . .  23
3-1  Types of Interventions Studied . . . . . . . . . . . . . . . . . . . . . . . .  55
3-2  Selected Characteristics of Research Sites . . . . . . . . . . . . . . . .  56
3-3  Additional Characteristics of Research Sites . . . . . . . . . . . . . .  59
4-1  Comparative Analysis of Six Work Place Interventions . . . . . .  76
4-2  Scanlon Plan Financial Data . . . . . . . . . . . . . . . . . . . . . . . . . .  99
4-3  Rucker Plan Productivity-Sharing Results . . . . . . . . . . . . . . .  100
4-4  Improshare Productivity Calculations . . . . . . . . . . . . . . . . . . .  103
5-1  Management and Union Responses to the Stimulus
     for Change and Cooperation . . . . . . . . . . . . . . . . . . . . . . . . .  113
5-2  Management and Union Responses to Process of Change . . . .  116
5-3  Design of Union-Management Interventions . . . . . . . . . . . . . .  119
5-4  Management and Union Perceptions
     of the Impact of Change . . . . . . . . . . . . . . . . . . . . . . . . . . . .  123
6-1  Summary of Intervention Impact on Performance . . . . . . . . . .  131
6-2  Bonus, Survival and Rater Effectiveness Summary . . . . . . . . .  133
6-3  Site 8 Summary . . . . . . . . . . . . . . . . . . . . . . . . . . . . . . . . . . . .  144
6-4  Site 4 Summary . . . . . . . . . . . . . . . . . . . . . . . . . . . . . . . . . . . .  149
6-5  Site 16 Summary . . . . . . . . . . . . . . . . . . . . . . . . . . . . . . . . . . .  153
6-6  Site 23 Summary . . . . . . . . . . . . . . . . . . . . . . . . . . . . . . . . . . .  163
6-7  Site 28 Bonus Summary . . . . . . . . . . . . . . . . . . . . . . . . . . . . . .  166
6-8  Sites 28, 30 and 9 Summary . . . . . . . . . . . . . . . . . . . . . . . . . . .  168
6-9  Sites 5 and 7 Summary . . . . . . . . . . . . . . . . . . . . . . . . . . . . . .  179
6-10 Site 6 Summary . . . . . . . . . . . . . . . . . . . . . . . . . . . . . . . . . . . .  184
6-11 Site 2 Summary . . . . . . . . . . . . . . . . . . . . . . . . . . . . . . . . . . . .  192
6-12 Sites 12, 13, 14 and 15 Summary . . . . . . . . . . . . . . . . . . . . . . .  208

# LIST OF FIGURES

2-1  Stages in the Cooperative Process: A Modification
     of the Kochan-Dyer Model .......................... 19
2-2  Nadler, Hanlon, and Lawler Model of Factors Influencing
     the Success of Labor-Management QWL Projects ......... 26
2-3  Goodman's Model of Scanlon Plan Effectiveness ........... 27
2-4  Steers Model of Commitment ......................... 31
2-5  A Model of Labor-Management Productivity
     Program Effectiveness .............................. 33
6-1  Site 8 Productivity ................................. 143
6-2  Site 16 Quality .................................... 154
6-3  Site 16 Absenteeism ............................... 155
6-4  Site 7 Productivity ................................. 180
6-5  Site 2 Employment ................................. 193
6-6  Site 12 Productivity ............................... 206
6-7  Site 13 Productivity ............................... 207

# Chapter 1

# Introduction

There is a long history of union-management cooperation in the United States. Although the resolution of important workplace issues continues to be most commonly addressed within the traditional system of collective bargaining, there is increasing evidence of a wide array of cooperative efforts taking place. These efforts are occurring within the immediate workplace as well as at company, industry, and national levels.[1]

Union-management cooperation can be classified into eight categories. At the macro level these have been: (1) *presidential labor-management committees* which were assembled during the Kennedy, Johnson, Nixon, Ford, and Carter presidencies. These committees differed in the scope of the agendas and in their prestige, but generally made recommendations on economic, industrial relations, and manpower issues (Maye 1980); (2) *industry level labor-management policy committees* (Driscoll 1980), for example the steel industry's human relations committee (Healy 1965) and those in retail food (Ray 1982) and health care (Corbett 1982); and (3) *joint industry or companywide committees to develop responses to technological change* (Brooks 1968; Healy 1965; Horvitz 1968; Shiron 1968).

At an intermediate level, (4) *areawide labor-management committees* developed during the 1970s (Ahern 1979; Leone, Eleey, Watkins, & Gershenfeld 1982; Popular 1980). Area

1

labor-management committees are composed of the community's key union leaders and chief operating managers. Most area committees employ a professional staff to direct their activities. Area committees sponsor social and educational events to increase communication and understanding between labor and management and to demonstrate the mutual benefits of cooperation, act as informal neutrals in difficult collective bargaining negotiations, and serve as an integral part of the area's economic development activities. The most important work of the area committees is in stimulating and facilitating the creation of in-plant labor-management committees to improve labor relations within establishments and, collectively, for the entire community.

At the plant level, four distinct efforts have appeared. Although several have overlapping goals, their structure and process are sufficiently distinct to require differential consideration. The four are: (5) *safety committees* (Beaumont & Deaton 1981; Kochan, Dyer & Lipsky 1977); (6) *in-plant labor-management committees and programs to improve union-management relations,* which have applied a variety of organizational development and other process change activities to reduce animosity and improve attitudes between unions and companies and to address problems normally outside the scope of traditional collective bargaining (Ahern 1978; Healy 1965; Mayer 1980). One such program was the Federal Mediation and Conciliation Service's Relationships-by-Objectives program (Gray, Sinicropi, & Hughes 1982); (7) *productivity committees, gainsharing or productivity plans, and quality circles* (Dale 1949; Dewar 1980; Dubin 1949; Fein 1981; Frost, Wakeley, & Ruh 1974; Lesieur 1958; Mohrman 1982; Moore & Goodman 1973; Moore & Ross 1978; Schuster 1983 a&b & 1984); and (8) efforts to improve *the quality of worklife* (Drexler & Lawler 1977; Goodman 1979; Macy 1979).

This book presents the findings of a five-year study of the structure, process, and impact of joint union-management programs to improve productivity. The focus of this research is on productivity-sharing plans[2] (PSPs) such as Scanlon, Rucker, and Improshare Plans, in-plant Labor-Management Committees (L-MCs), Quality Circles (QCs), and Quality of Worklife (QWL) projects.[3] *All of the programs have a common basis, that is, they are structural interventions which attempt to generate greater worker interest, involvement and effort toward achieving important organization goals.*

In spite of the long history of union-management cooperation, there has been very little scientific analysis of the structure, process, and impact of cooperative programs. The dominant form of research in the field has been case analysis. Empirical studies have tended to be mostly attitudinal. This research breaks new ground in three areas. First, it is a large sample (38 sites) of firms with cooperative union-management programs. Second, the research utilized actual performance measures, for example, of productivity. And finally, the research employed a longitudinal research design along with sophisticated analytical methods. Thus this research offers both substantive findings on the structure, process, and impact of union-management cooperation (chapters 4, 5, 6) as well as addressing and developing methodological techniques for evaluating cooperative programs (chapter 3).

This introductory chapter is divided into three sections. At the outset a section underscoring the growth and importance of union-management cooperation is presented. This is followed by a discussion of union and management attitudes toward cooperation. The third section is a brief description of the structure of the book.

## Importance of Union-Management Cooperation

It is unlikely that change in the American industrial relations system would have occurred in the absence of sweeping environmental influences. Since the early 1970s, foreign competition, the increased cost advantages and more modern equipment of the nonunion sector of the economy, and a change in the values, attitudes, and work behaviors of much of the labor force have increasingly shaken the foundations of the traditional system of collective bargaining. In more recent years, harsh economic difficulties have accelerated the process of change and accommodation. Whether, and to what degree, the increased levels of cooperation will continue once economic conditions stabilize is very much an open question. At the present time, however, companies have had to increase their efficiency in order to remain viable, and one strategy for doing so has been to expand the level of employee and union involvement in decisionmaking affecting the workplace. Many of these efforts were stimulated and publicized by the now defunct National Center for Productivity and the Quality of Working Life (NCPQWL).

Although there is no way of knowing precisely how much cooperation is occurring in the United States, there is evidence which suggests that there has been a marked increase in cooperative activities. This evidence comes from a variety of governmental, academic, and journalistic sources. In 1977 and 1978, the NCPQWL published directories listing companies and unions with ongoing cooperative activities. In each case, approximately 100 experiments were listed. The publication of the directory was suspended until the 1982 edition, published by the U.S. Department of Labor, which contains a listing of 700 experiments.

Additional evidence of the upswing in cooperative labor-management activity may be found in the increase in safety committees. The Bureau of National Affairs has reported that in its 1979 survey of collective bargaining agreements, 43 percent contained provisions calling for safety committees. This was an increase in the number of contracts with such provisions over the 1970 and 1975 surveys which reported 31 percent and 39 percent, respectively.

In a recent study of 26 sites with labor-management committees in Illinois, Derber and Flanigan (1980) found that the majority had been established in the 1970s. Moreover, five were found to be revitalized efforts of earlier years.

During the 1970s, the number of area labor-management committees increased to just over 20. Although several communities—Toledo, Ohio (1945) and Louisville, Kentucky—already had such committees, it was the success of the Jamestown, New York committee (1972) which drew significant attention. The increasing use of areawide labor-management committees represents the development of an important new institutional arrangement in industrial relations.

There is no precise way of knowing how many Scanlon, Rucker, and Improshare Plans, profit-sharing plans, quality circles, or quality of worklife programs have been instituted. However, a 1982 survey by the New York Stock Exchange (NYSE) highlights the growth of workplace changes. The NYSE (1982) study was based on a sample of 49,000 corporations with one hundred or more employees. The study reported the "most rapidly growing human resource activities over the past two years" (p. 26). Over the two-year reporting period, the following efforts were initiated: 74 percent added quality circles, 36 percent job design/redesign, 30 percent group incentive plans, and 29 percent production teams. There is other qualitative evidence which strongly suggests increasingly widespread use of these cooperative strategies. First, there has been overwhelming attention in the popular press to companies with quality circles, gainsharing programs and quality of worklife efforts. *Business Week* titled its special report on these efforts "The New Industrial Relations." Second, there is evidence that the use of these strategies has spread from the traditional manufacturing sector into the service and public sectors. Finally, there have been several important national bargaining agreements (for example in auto, steel, and communications) which encompass one or more cooperative strategies.

These efforts have taken on a new sense of urgency and importance as demonstrated by the recently enacted Labor-Management Cooperation Act (LMCA) of 1978 [29 U.S.C. 1975(a)]. The LMCA is designed to encourage plant, area, and industrywide cooperative union-management efforts to:

(1) improve communication between representatives of labor and management;

(2) provide workers and employers with opportunities to study and explore new and innovative joint approaches to achieving organizational effectiveness;

(3) assist workers and employers in solving problems of mutual concern not susceptible to resolution within the collective bargaining process;

(4) study and explore ways of eliminating potential problems which reduce the competitiveness and inhibit the economic development of the plant, area, or industry;

(5) enhance the involvement of workers in making decisions that affect their working lives;

(6) expand and improve working relationships between workers and managers; and

(7) encourage free collective bargaining by establishing continuing mechanisms for communication between employers and their employees through Federal assistance to the formation and operation of labor-management committees.

The Federal Mediation and Conciliation Service (FMCS) has been empowered to provide financial and technical assistance to aid companies and unions in this process. Limited amounts of funds have been allocated by the FMCS, most of it going to support area labor-management committees.

Three studies by the United States General Accounting Office (GAO) also underscore the potential importance of this subject. The first GAO (1980a) study criticized the now defunct Council on Wage and Price Stability for its failure to promulgate an exemption to its compensation standards for pay increases associated with productivity-sharing plans such as Scanlon, Rucker, and Improshare.

The second study (GAO 1980b) criticized the United States Department of Labor for not having expended resources or provided sufficient leadership to encourage improvements in workers' productivity in the private sector. The GAO recommended that the Department of Labor develop programs and encourage human resource efforts to improve productivity. Finally, the third study (GAO 1981) of productivity-sharing plans found that they had had a positive impact on organizational productivity as well as improving labor-management relations, reducing absenteeism, turnover, and grievances.

In September 1982, the U.S. Department of Labor, in a departure from past policy, announced the formation of a new division, the Cooperative Labor-Management Programs Division, to encourage shop floor cooperation. The initial mission of the Division will be limited to the gathering and dissemination of information. Yet, this represents a first step in federal recognition and support for change at the workplace.

It is somewhat paradoxical that the increase in cooperative activity in the United States comes at a time when relations between the labor movement and employers at the national level have been strained. Increased employer aggressiveness in political activity and at the workplace, as well as an anti-union administration in Washington, have caused this rift.

In the political arena, employer lobbying resulted in the defeat of Common Situs Picketing and Labor Law Reform legislation. Both of these bills were actively sought by the labor movement. At the workplace there has been increased management opposition to union efforts to organize non-union operations, as well as increased efforts to decertify existing unions. In collective bargaining, management demands for concessions on wages and work rules have been widespread.

The apparent dichotomy between conflict at the national level and cooperation at the plant level can be explained by the strong stimulus for change being created by the harsh economic environment faced by many firms, thus providing the requisite stimuli to shape local collective bargaining relations, national activity notwithstanding.

### Union and Management Attitudes Toward Cooperation

Large scale studies of union and management attitudes toward cooperation have not been undertaken. Two studies, however, one by Kochan, Lipsky, & Dyer (1974) and another commissioned by *Business Week* ("Concessionary Bargaining" June 14, 1982) and conducted by Louis Harris & Associates do provide some evidence of attitudes toward cooperation. The Kochan, Lipsky & Dyer study surveyed a sample of local and district level union leaders as well as stewards and committee members. Their results are summarized in table 1-1.

Union activists were found to support cooperative strategies on some workplace issues. The respondents were questioned as to their rating of the effectiveness of collective bargaining in handling 13 work-related issues. The majority of the respondents indicated that collective bargaining was "somewhat helpful" or "very helpful" in resolving issues related to fringe benefits (91 percent); earnings (90 percent); job security (80 percent); grievance procedures (76 percent);

## Table 1-1
## Union Attitudes Toward Cooperation

| Issue | Respondents' ratings of effectiveness of collective bargaining | | Respondents' opinions about "best way" to deal with issues | | |
|---|---|---|---|---|---|
| | Not very helpful/ not helpful at all | Somewhat helpful/ very helpful | Set up a joint program with management | Seek improvements through formal bargaining | Should not get involved |
| Interesting work | 74.5 | 25.5 | 67.8 | 16.3 | 15.9 |
| Supervisors | 68.9 | 31.1 | 65.6 | 19.3 | 15.1 |
| Control of work | 67.3 | 32.7 | 53.8 | 26.9 | 19.3 |
| Productivity | 61.7 | 38.2 | 51.2 | 25.1 | 23.7 |
| Better job | 63.0 | 37.0 | 38.4 | 43.6 | 18.0 |
| Adequate resources | 57.7 | 42.3 | 60.6 | 21.2 | 17.8 |
| Work load | 54.5 | 45.5 | 43.8 | 42.3 | 13.9 |
| Hours | 41.8 | 58.3 | 31.1 | 65.6 | 3.3 |
| Safety | 35.1 | 64.9 | 41.1 | 56.5 | 2.4 |
| Grievance procedures | 24.1 | 75.8 | 32.7 | 67.3 | 0.0 |
| Job security | 20.2 | 79.8 | 12.2 | 85.9 | 1.9 |
| Earnings | 10.4 | 89.6 | 5.6 | 93.9 | 0.5 |
| Fringe benefits | 9.5 | 90.5 | 4.2 | 95.5 | 0.5 |

Adapted from Kochan, Lipsky & Dyer (1974).

safety (65 percent); and hours (58 percent). At the same time collective bargaining was found to be "not very helpful" or "not helpful at all" in addressing interesting work (76 percent); supervisors (68 percent); control of work (67 percent); productivity (62 percent); better job (63 percent); adequate resources (58 percent); and work load (55 percent).

The respondents were then asked what the "best way" was to deal with the issues. More than half the respondents would "seek improvements through formal collective bargaining" for issues of fringe benefits (96 percent), earnings (94 percent), job security (86 percent), hours (66 percent), grievance procedures (67 percent), and safety (57 percent). However, there was a distinct preference for setting up "a joint program with management outside collective bargaining" for interesting work (68 percent), supervisors (66 percent), adequate resources (61 percent), control of work (54 percent), and productivity (51 percent). Only on the issue of work load did the respondents split (44 percent for joint program, 42 percent through collective bargaining). These results were replicated by Ponak and Fraser (1979) on a sample of Canadian trade unionists with similar results.

According to the union activists, collective bargaining was viewed as effective in resolving more traditional issues—wages, fringe benefits, and grievances. Thus, there was less preference for collaboration with management. Collective bargaining was viewed as less effective in resolving issues related to productivity and the quality of worklife and there was greater interest expressed in pursuing joint programs. Although clear policy preferences emerge from this study, it is difficult to ascertain whether these differences are translated into practice.

At the national level, union officials have spoken out on the issue of cooperation with varying degrees of enthusiasm. Glenn Watts, president of the Communications Workers Union of America is a proponent of cooperation. He states:

Labor is concerned with the development of democracy in Industry. The collective bargaining process will always be the foundation of industrial democracy; but QWL gives us the tools to build higher than we ever have before.

For our Members, QWL has provided one of the most important benefits of all—the chance to be treated with dignity and have a voice on the job.

. . . through QWL, we are extending our influence into the murky territory of 'management prerogatives,' helping to shape management practices and policies while they are being formed rather than after the fact. (Watts 1982)

Thus, consistent with the views of local activists, Watts sees cooperative strategies as supplementing union efforts through collective bargaining and being primarily responsive to nontraditional issues such as the nature of the work and the relationship between supervision and workers.

A different view of QWL programs was recently taken by George J. Poulin, general vice-president of the International Association of Machinists and Aerospace Workers (Poulin 1982). An extensive portion of his statement is reproduced here because it reflects a view of cooperation that has not received sufficient attention.

If the shop floor people are so vital in achieving management's goals—in providing the benefits just listed [improved worker job satisfaction, improved product quality, reduced unit labor costs by increasing productivity]—then why in the hell hasn't management recognized our vitality, until now?

All of a sudden, why is it that *we* start sharing in decisions?

Our quick answer is that management has often made such a mess of things, they want to share the blame. They come to us, *after* they've screwed up.

A second answer is that management wants to make a change in production planning or process, or it wants to introduce some new technology—either or both of which will shove some of us out the door onto the unemployment line—and it wants to con us into helping get the job done.

A third answer is management simply wants more production—more work—from the same or fewer workers. In other words, a speed up.

But a fourth answer is more likely the real answer: To undercut the union; to use up its duties and powers and responsibilities; to make it seem unnecessary and ultimately put it out of business; to take control of workers away from the bargaining agent and put in the grip of management itself.

Poulin argues that the goals of QWL programs can be accomplished through the existing collective agreements.

It is too early to determine whether the Watts or Poulin view best describes the eventual outcome of cooperation. It will take more time, experience with cooperation, and evaluation research to determine whether meaningful change has come about from cooperation and whether cooperative strategies have enabled unions to better represent their members. For the time being, however, cooperative strategies continue to increase, but the future will be largely determined by the manner in which the parties manage the current level of cooperation.

Management attitudes toward cooperation were assessed in a survey of more than 400 "high-level executives" of large companies reported by *Business Week* ("Concessionary

Bargaining'' 1982). Executives were asked whether they would like to see a return to traditional bargaining once the economy became healthy or whether they would prefer giving unions and workers more say in company operations if employee compensation were tied to company performance. Overall, 50 percent of the executives would opt for greater union and employee involvement. The complete results of the survey, along with a breakdown by the extent of unionization and industry, are presented in table 1-2.

Heavily unionized companies were more likely to favor employee participation than firms which have experienced unionization to a lesser degree. The number favoring participation increased from 42 percent to 58 percent as the degree of unionization in the company increased from 40 percent or fewer to more than 70 percent of employees. There were also differences among various industry groups with utilities (87 percent) and electrical (73 percent) most heavily favoring cooperation and natural resources (27 percent) and retail (25 percent) least likely to prefer cooperation.

Although not a pure indication of management preference, the data still suggest a change in traditional management attitudes. When combined with the growing emphasis on employee involvement strategies discussed in the previous section, it must be concluded that a significant shift has occurred in management's approach to workplace collaboration.

## Structure of the Book

The main body of this monograph is organized into six chapters. Chapter 2 presents an overview of theories and models of cooperation and change in unionized settings. The overview is followed by the models employed to guide this research, the specific research issues treated, and the justification for each aspect of the study. Chapter 3 provides

## Table 1-2
## Management Attitudes Toward Cooperation

|  | Total | Size of company | | | Unionization | | |
|---|---|---|---|---|---|---|---|
|  |  | Top third | Middle third | Bottom third | 1 - 40% | 41 - 70% | 71 - 100% |
| Total answer | 427 100% | 136 100% | 144 100% | 138 100% | 198 100% | 110 100% | 107 100% |
| More of say for unions and workers | 211 50% | 68 50% | 67 47% | 70 51% | 83 42% | 61 56% | 62 58% |
| Traditional adversary relationship | 146 34% | 38 28% | 52 36% | 54 39% | 80 40% | 30 27% | 33 31% |
| Not sure | 70 16% | 30 22% | 25 17% | 14 10% | 35 18% | 19 17% | 12 11% |

|  | Industry group | | | | | | | | |
|---|---|---|---|---|---|---|---|---|---|
|  | Banks | Electrical | Food | Misc. manu. | Retail nonfood | Service ind. | Textiles | Utilities | Natural resources |
| Total answer | -- -- | 11 100% | 26 100% | 44 100% | 16 100% | 43 100% | 12 100% | 8 100% | 22 100% |
| More of say for unions and workers | -- -- | 8 73% | 10 38% | 24 54% | 4 25% | 23 53% | 6 50% | 7 87% | 6 27% |
| Traditional adversary relationship | -- -- | 3 27% | 12 47% | 10 23% | 10 62% | 14 33% | 5 42% | 1 13% | 11 50% |
| Not sure | -- -- | -- -- | 4 15% | 10 23% | 2 13% | 6 14% | 1 8% | -- -- | 5 23% |

SOURCE: Unpublished data provided to the author by *Business Week*.

a detailed presentation of the research design, measures of study variables, and analytical techniques employed, as well as a summary of the characteristics of the research sites and methodological findings. Chapters 4-6 present the findings from this research. Chapters 4 and 5 are, of necessity, more qualitative and descriptive, while chapter 6 includes both quantitative and case study evidence. Chapter 4 describes the structural characteristics of the six types of interventions studied. This includes not only the findings from the immediate work, but also draws from the literature to provide a more thorough overview. Chapter 5 deals with the results of the process leading to cooperation and some of the conditions necessary to implement and maintain a cooperative program.

In chapter 6, the results of the analysis of performance at the research sites are presented. Although the type and duration of the data on each site varies, there is a substantial amount of data on productivity and employment and lesser amounts on quality, turnover, absenteeism, and grievances. Some of the time-series data sets on these variables are as long as eight years, making this the first truly longitudinal study on this subject matter. Chapter 6 also includes 11 case studies which serve to highlight significant issues involved in the practice of cooperative union-management relations. In chapter 7, a summary of the research methodology and the findings is offered, along with a future research agenda.

## NOTES

1. One of the most comprehensive works on cooperation and change is by Irving H. Siegel and Edgar Weinberg, *Labor-Management Cooperation: The American Experience.* Kalamazoo, MI: The W.E. Upjohn Institute for Employment Research, 1982.

2. In recent years, productivity-sharing plans have oftentimes been referred to as gainsharing plans. The terms are used synonymously.

3. Most readers will be familiar with these six types of interventions. Those readers wishing more information on the types of programs studied should refer to chapter 4.

# Chapter 2

# Models of Change and Cooperation in Unionized Settings

The outcomes of collective bargaining are generally considered to form a web of rules to govern the workplace (Dunlop 1958). The interaction of labor and management in traditional conflict-based bargaining is the mechanism which drives the system of industrial relations. In this system, bargaining power, defined as "the ability to secure another's agreement on one's own terms" (Chamberlain & Kuhn 1965, p. 170) is paramount. Each side considers the costs of agreeing and disagreeing with its opponent and develops a strategy for rendering economic harm and defending against economic attack. Strikes, picketing, boycotts, stockpiling, strike funds, etc. are the gears of the collective bargaining system.

Other forms and processes of bargaining have been identified and categorized within the traditional process by Walton and McKersie (1965). Thus integrative or problem-solving bargaining, attitudinal structuring or the relationship between the employer and the labor organization, as well as the relationship between the key union and management actors, and intraorganizational bargaining or the relationships and internal political considerations *within* each organization, serve to underscore the complexity of the traditional process.

17

It is within this framework that cooperation and change must occur. Through the years, the occasional necessity to cooperate rather than confront has forced labor and management to approach their relationship in a different way. The difficult economic times since the early 1970s and changing work attitudes and behaviors on the part of the workforce have stimulated the need for change. As demonstrated in the previous chapter, union leaders and managers now show increased support for cooperative programs to resolve issues of productivity and improve the quality of worklife (Dyer, Lipsky & Kochan 1977; Kochan, Lipsky & Dyer 1974; Ponak & Fraser 1979).

## Models of Change and Cooperation

Although not all of the propositions have been identified and ordered, five models of change and cooperation in unionized settings have been developed. Kochan and Dyer's (1976) model integrates the organizational change and industrial relations literature into a general three-stage (stimulus for change, initial commitment, and institutionalization of the change) model for change. Lawler and Drexler (1978) have analyzed the dynamics of establishing cooperative union-management quality of worklife projects and identified the factors operating in favor of, and against such efforts. Three other models have addressed the variables necessary to operationally succeed in implementing cooperative programs. Nadler, Hanlon, and Lawler (1980) have identified the factors influencing the success of labor-management quality of worklife projects. Goodman (1973) has proposed an expectancy model to explain Scanlon Plan performance, which probably has applicability to all gain-sharing programs. Finally, a model of labor-management productivity program effectiveness (Schuster 1980) was developed to guide this research. The Schuster model is broadly based and was designed to be useful in studying all forms of cooperative programs having a goal of improved productivity and increased organizational effectiveness. This would include gainsharing, as well as quality circles, labor-management committees and quality of worklife projects.

All of these models are complementary. The first four will be discussed in this section since they provided useful guidance to the study of cooperation and many variables and issues suggested by their developers were examined as part of this research. The effectiveness model will be presented in the next section which outlines the hypotheses investigated in this study.

Figure 2-1 outlines the stages of the cooperative process by modifying the Kochan-Dyer model to encompass a fourth stage (third in time), program operational success. This permits a visual integration of all the models.

**Figure 2-1**
**Stages in the Cooperative Process: A Modification**
**of the Kochan-Dyer Model**

| One | Two | Three | Four |
| --- | --- | --- | --- |
| Stimuli | Initial Decision | Program Opera-tional Success | Institutionalization into the ongoing L-M |
| Kochan-Dyer Model; Lawler-Drexler Model; | | Goodman Model; Nadler, Hanlon, Lawler Model; Schuster Model; | Kochan-Dyer Model |

## Lawler-Drexler Model

Lawler and Drexler enumerated the factors working for and against joint union-management quality of worklife projects. Table 2-1 summarizes their work.

**Table 2-1**
**Summary of Factors Working For and Against**
**Joint Union-Management QWL Projects**

## Union-Management QWL Projects

| Factors working in favor | Factors working against |
|---|---|
| 1. QWL project would be more effective if cooperatively directed | 1. Goal conflict<br>  a) Union—employment security, higher wages and benefits, job rights<br>  b) Management—profit, productivity, organizational effectiveness |
| 2. Reduces resistance to change | 2. Lack of a model to structure projects |
| 3. Change will be more sustainable | 3. Lack of knowledge about organizational change, development, and psychology; job redesign |
| 4. Avoid legislation imposing collaboration | 4. Long-standing adversary relationship |
| 5. Union can achieve noneconomic benefits for members | 5. Potential loss of power for managers and union leaders |
| 6. Reduces adversary nature of relationship | 6. Impact on collective bargaining agreement; modification of traditional clauses |
| | 7. Time involved for planning and implementation |
| | 8. Differing expectations of project outcomes |
| | 9. Obtaining qualified consultants |

SOURCE: Lawler & Drexler (1978).

The Lawler-Drexler model accurately lists the reasons why union-management collaboration is not only desirable, but necessary. It would seem inconceivable that major organizational change could be effectively implemented in a unionized setting without union involvement or tacit approval. However, there are still instances where management attempts to bring about change without consultation or approval of the union which represents its employees. Union involvement not only reduces resistance to change, but provides greater acceptance of it, and can stimulate further change.

Some unions have come to view cooperative strategies as a complementary, rather than competing avenue for improving the welfare of their members. According to Glenn Watts, president of the Communications Workers of America, quality of worklife programs lead to:

> . . . lasting improvements in job satisfaction among union members. And I believe if we respond to the challenge posed by QWL, it offers us in the Labor Movement the opportunity to deal with many issues which have been beyond the reach of traditional collective agreement. (Watts 1982)

Many Americans will no doubt question the suggestion that voluntary joint QWL programs will avoid legislation imposing collaboration. But just such a legislative scheme is under discussion in the European Parliament: the draft Fifth Directive and Vredeling draft Directive would impose forms of employee participation, information sharing, and consultation in the member countries of the European Economic Community. Although similar provisions would not seem on the horizon in the United States, successful voluntary efforts would continue to reduce the likelihood of imposed collaboration.

The factors working against joint involvement are more in the nature of obstacles to be overcome. Readers should consider the items in this listing since many of the interventions reported in this research were less effective or not effective at all because of the failure to agree on goals, differing expectations, lack of qualified consultants, and failure to reduce the adversary nature of the parties' relationship.

## Kochan-Dyer Model

Kochan-Dyer's model was the first effort to conceptualize the change and cooperative process in union-management settings. In contrast to the Lawler-Drexler work, the Kochan-Dyer integration of the organizational change and industrial relations literature is conceptualized into a series of testable hypotheses. As will be discussed further in the next section, one aspect of this research was to collect data to explore the validity of the Kochan-Dyer model. In chapter 5, some preliminary data on this model are presented.

Underlying the Kochan-Dyer model are three assumptions. First, that there are sets of interests (individuals, employer, and union) created as a result of the union-management relationship which are accepted as legitimate by the others. These interests are interdependent and each party pursues its own goals through a series of interactions within the context of this interdependent relationship. Second, because of the protections afforded unions in the society, competing organizations must share power. Third, since their respective goals are somewhat incompatible, this inevitably results in structurally-based conflict. The Kochan-Dyer model is summarized in table 2-2.

In the first stage of their model, Kochan and Dyer hypothesize that the parties will consider a joint venture only when there is strong internal or external stimulus for change. An internal stimulus is an outgrowth of the parties' previous interaction or a current workplace problem. Some examples of an internal stimulus include a bitter strike, distressed grievance procedure, high accident rates or a series of ac-

**Table 2-2**
**Summary of the Kochan-Dyer Model of Organizational Change**
**in the Context of Union-Management Relations**

| Stage | | Factor | Outcome |
|---|---|---|---|
| One | (a) | Greater internal pressure | Consider joint venture |
| | (b) | Greater external pressure | |
| Stimuli | (c) | Less effective formal bargaining process | |
| Two | (d) | Perceive change as being instrumental | Embark on specific change program |
| | (e) | Parties negotiate/compromise over goals | |
| Initial decision to participate | (f) | No attempt to block program by coalitions or individual power holders | |
| Three | (g) | Valued goals achieved in initial phase | Mutual commitment to maintain program |
| | (h) | High probability valued goals achieved in future | |
| Maintain commitment over time | (i) | Initial goals not displaced by goals of higher priority | |
| | (j) | Program stimulus remains strong | |
| | (k) | Equitable distribution of benefits | |
| | (l) | Union perceived as instrumental in attaining program benefits | |
| | (m) | Program not infringing on traditional collective bargaining issues | |
| | (n) | Program doesn't threaten management prerogatives | |
| | (o) | Program not overlapping jurisdiction of grievance procedure | |
| | (p) | Union leaders not viewed as being co-opted | |
| | (q) | Program protected from use of bargaining tactics and maneuvers | |
| | (r) | Union leaders continue to pursue member goals on distributive issues | |

SOURCE: Kochan & Dyer (1976).

cidents, technological change, low productivity, and problems of absenteeism, alcoholism, and substance abuse. External stimuli develop outside the realm of the parties' interaction. Some examples of external stimuli include federal legislation governing occupational safety and health, equal employment opportunity, and pension reform, as well as foreign and domestic competition. A strong stimulus can reduce goal conflict as the parties may come to view cooperation as increasing their ability to maximize their joint outcomes. In other words, *environmental factors may force the parties to cooperate in order to avoid the difficulties that would occur if they did not cooperate.*

Because of traditional hostility toward joint union-management programs, the parties will first look to the traditional collective bargaining process for relief, regardless of whether the stimulus is internal or external. This is appropriate in view of the fact that most union leaders and members of labor unions tend to view collective bargaining as the primary mechanism for resolving problems. Managers also tend to avoid many cooperative strategies for fear that collaboration might reduce management prerogatives. It is presumed that if the traditional process is capable of dealing adequately with the issues raised by the stimulus, there will be no need for organizational change.

Stage Two of the model addresses the factors which move the parties from an initial decision to participate in the change program to a commitment to embark upon a specific change effort. The program must be viewed as being instrumental, agreed-upon goals must be established, and there must be no attempt by coalitions to block the program.

Stage Three concerns program maintenance. Mutual commitment to maintain the program over time (Stage Three) is said to occur when valued goals are achieved in the initial phase of the effort; there is a high probability of valued goals being achieved in the future; initial goals are not displaced by goals of a higher priority; the program stimulus remains strong; there is equitable distribution of the benefits; the union is seen as being instrumental in attaining program benefits; the program does not infringe on traditional collective bargaining issues or overlap the grievance procedure; the program doesn't threaten management prerogatives and the union leadership is not viewed as being co-opted; and the program is protected from the use of bargaining tactics or maneuvers, while the union leadership continues to pursue member goals on distributive issues.

## Nadler, Hanlon, and Lawler Model

Nadler, Hanlon, and Lawler's model combines two factors (ownership of the project and goals) associated with the Lawler-Drexler and Kochan-Dyer models. However, it also breaks new ground by adding four operational and contextual variables including consultant effectiveness, labor-management committee functioning, organizational climate, and organizational financial viability. Figure 2-2 outlines their model and the correlation coefficients between these variables and project effectiveness.

The data to test this model were collected at a conference of union, management, and rank-and-file workers involved in ongoing QWL projects. Project effectiveness was defined as improvements in quality of work, organizational functioning and a global success measure. Self-report measures were used to assess all the measures. In spite of this limitation and a relatively small sample (N = 64), this study presents useful data on cooperative program effectiveness.

It is interesting to note that a good labor-management relationship within the organization and on the labor-management steering committee were related to QWL project effectiveness. Later on it will be suggested that a good labor-management relationship may be a precondition to change. The importance of employing an effective consul-

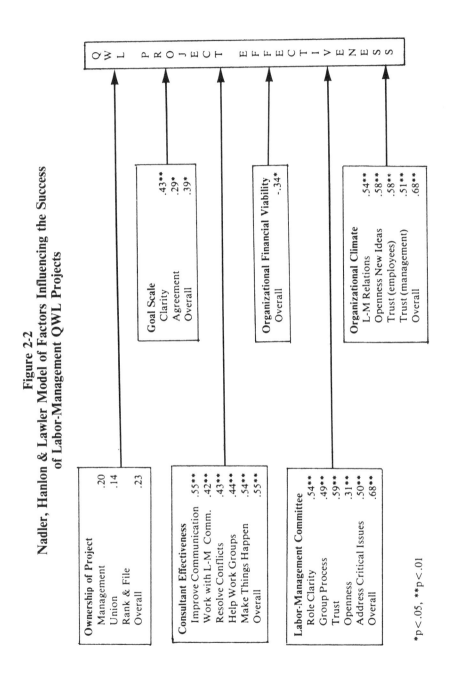

**Figure 2-2**
**Nadler, Hanlon & Lawler Model of Factors Influencing the Success**
**of Labor-Management QWL Projects**

| | |
|---|---|
| **Ownership of Project** | |
| Management | .20 |
| Union | .14 |
| Rank & File | |
| Overall | .23 |

| | |
|---|---|
| **Consultant Effectiveness** | |
| Improve Communication | .55** |
| Work with L-M Comm. | .42** |
| Resolve Conflicts | .43** |
| Help Work Groups | .44** |
| Make Things Happen | .54** |
| Overall | .55** |

| | |
|---|---|
| **Labor-Management Committee** | |
| Role Clarity | .54** |
| Group Process | .49** |
| Trust | .59** |
| Openness | .31** |
| Address Critical Issues | .50** |
| Overall | .68** |

| | |
|---|---|
| **Goal Scale** | |
| Clarity | .43** |
| Agreement | .29* |
| Overall | .39* |

| | |
|---|---|
| **Organizational Financial Viability** | |
| Overall | -.34* |

| | |
|---|---|
| **Organizational Climate** | |
| L-M Relations | .54** |
| Openness New Ideas | .58** |
| Trust (employees) | .58** |
| Trust (management) | .51** |
| Overall | .68** |

QWL PROJECT EFFECTIVENESS

*p<.05, **p<.01

tant is also underscored. Financial viability was hypothesized to be related to project effectiveness since financial resources are required to make QWL programs successful. These include monies for staff, consultants, time off for committee meetings, travel to conferences, etc. Yet financial viability was shown to be negatively related to the success of the project. Nadler, Hanlon & Lawler (1980) suggest that there may be a curvilinear relationship, that is, where there are resources available for experimentation and where cooperation is needed to insure survival.

## Goodman's Model of Scanlon Plan Effectiveness

Goodman has offered an expectancy model to predict Scanlon Plan success. Figure 2-3 outlines his model, which would also seem applicable to other forms of gainsharing.

**Figure 2-3**
**Goodman's Model of Scanlon Plan Effectiveness**
(Reprinted with permission)

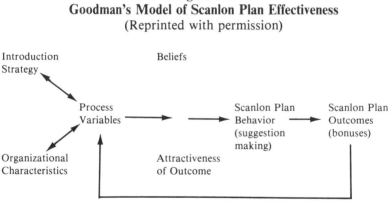

The expectancy component of Goodman's model considers the effect of individual differences in the attractiveness of Scanlon outcomes (bonuses) and individual beliefs on increased efforts (harder work, suggestion-making) that will lead to those desired outcomes. These are enclosed in the box in figure 2-3. Process variables, such as the reinforcement effect from the bonus or social reinforcement, are seen as influencing beliefs about the plan. Finally, the structural and environmental characteristics of the organization such as the task structure, superior-subordinate relationships, work group structure, labor-management relations, and financial condition are suggested to influence the process variables. It is noteworthy that Goodman treats the Scanlon Plan outcome as the bonus. This is certainly a significant part of the Scanlon Plan. However, it could also be argued that the change in management style, the opportunity to become involved in workplace decisions, and changes in subordinate-supervisory relations also constitute employee outcomes. Therefore, it may be that the expectancy model is even more appropriate to the other gainsharing plans (Rucker and Improshare) where there is greater emphasis on financial rewards than to the Scanlon Plan.

## Research Objectives

This research investigated the structure, process, and impact of joint union-management programs. This section contains the research issues and hypotheses which served to focus the research. Many aspects of the study were approached as research issues rather than as testable hypotheses for two reasons. First, the strategy appeared to be consistent with the case study approach and would permit an in-depth descriptive analysis. Second, although the sample of firms was large in relation to previous studies on this topic, it was not believed to be sufficiently large to permit testing of all the hypotheses. Thus in the structural (chapter 4) and process (chapter 5) portions of the study an attempt was made to measure the presence of many characteristics identified in the change models. Chapter 6, the impact portion, includes both quantitative and case study analyses.

## Program Structure Research Issues

The program structure segment analyses the case study information as well as reviewing the literature on each program. This portion of the study represents an attempt to engage in a comparative analysis of six widely used union-management interventions—Scanlon, Rucker, and Improshare Plans, Quality Circles, Labor-Management Committees, and Quality of Worklife Projects. The following aspects of program structure are considered.

(1) program philosophy/theory
(2) primary goals of the program
(3) subsidiary goals of the program
(4) structure for worker participation
(5) mechanism for employee suggestion-making
(6) role of supervision
(7) role of management
(8) productivity-sharing formulas
(9) frequency of payout
(10) role of union
(11) impact on management style

One of the overall findings of this research was that all the programs can be successful in some settings and ineffective in others. Moreover, in practice the "standard design" for each program became diluted and modified due to local necessity or preferences. The chapter on structure, which is entirely descriptive, should be very useful to students, managers, union leaders, and policymakers in comparing the merits and utility of each program.

## Cooperative Process Research Issues

The segment on the cooperative process involved the collection of data on the process of change and perceptions of cooperation. The Kochan-Dyer model provided the direction for most of this part of the research. Data were collected which permitted an assessment of the propensity of each factor in their change model to occur in actual experience. Additional process data predominantly related to other change models were also collected. Thus, the report contains information on:

(1)  the stimulus for change
(2)  the process of change
   (a)  the efforts made to resolve stimulus issues in traditional bargaining
   (b)  the incidence of opposition coalitions to block the change effort
   (c)  the use and role of neutrals or consultants
   (d)  the expected utility of the program to address the stimulus issues
(3)  the operational issues in the design of change programs
   (a)  the overlap, if any, with the grievance procedure and the collective bargaining process
   (b)  the presence of job security guarantees
   (c)  opportunities for employee participation
   (d)  training for supervisors to implement the program
   (e)  changes in skills-based training programs
   (f)  bonus sharing procedures
(4)  union-management perceptions of the impact of change on
   (a)  overall union-management relations
   (b)  union-management relations on productivity issues
   (c)  the union's role in productivity improvement
   (d)  management's commitment to productivity improvement

The data were compiled from questionnaires completed by management representatives and local union presidents. Additional qualitative data were derived from open-ended interview questions and internal documents.

## A Model of Labor-Management Productivity Program Effectiveness

A model of labor-management productivity program effectiveness was developed from the investigation of the first 10 research sites (Schuster 1980). The driving variable in this model is employee commitment. According to Steers (1977), commitment is operationalized as:

(1) A strong belief in, and acceptance of, the organization's goals and values;
(2) A willingness to exert considerable effort on behalf of the organization;
(3) A strong desire to maintain membership in the organization.

Steers' model is presented in figure 2-4.

**Figure 2-4**
**Steers Model of Commitment**

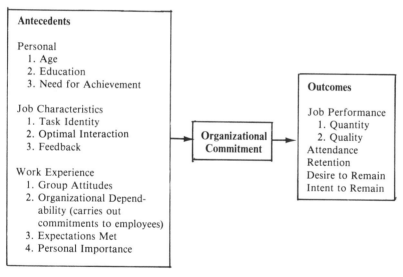

---

Reprinted from "Antecedents and Outcomes of Organizational Commitment by Richard M. Steers in *Administrative Science Quarterly,* 22(1) by permission of *Administrative Science Quarterly.*

As noted in the introduction, all six cooperative union-management programs are structural interventions which attempt to generate greater worker interest, involvement and effort toward achieving important organization goals. Thus the conceptualization of commitment is congruent with the underlying theory of each intervention. In addition, the outcomes/results of the employee commitment model reflect the goals of the interventions. The interventions are designed to have a positive impact on job performance and to improve work attitudes and behavior. Finally, the antecedents of commitment, particularly the need for achievement, task identity, optimal interaction, feedback, group attitudes, organizational dependability, and personal importance are many of the conditions the union-management programs attempt to establish and enhance.

Although there was no previous empirical evidence to suggest that Steer's commitment model, Kochan-Dyer's model of change, Goodman's expectancy model, or some other construct explained the success or failure of the interventions, these were believed to provide a solid foundation upon which to base this investigation.[1] The model developed to guide this research, presented in figure 2-5, accepts the Kochan-Dyer logic that cooperation is based upon a stimulus for change. Thereafter, union and company commitment will occur if the traditional collective bargaining process is ineffective at addressing the stimulus issues, change is perceived as being instrumental to resolution of the stimulus issues, the parties are able to agree on program goals, and there is no attempt to block the cooperative effort by coalitions or individual power holders. The nature of the stimulus can influence organizational commitment. For example, severe economic difficulties were more likely to bring about commitment to change than simply a desire to change the payment system.

Organizational values are thought to influence or moderate the manner in which the parties interpret the

**Figure 2-5**
**A Model of Labor-Management Productivity Program Effectiveness**
(Schuster 1980)

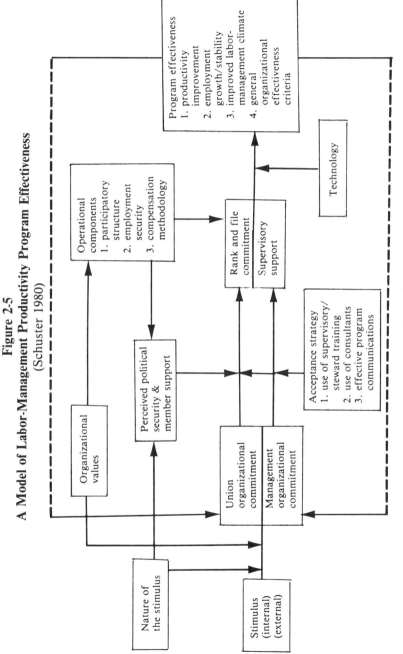

stimulus variables. When faced with a difficult economic situation, some companies will take an extremely hard-line position, while others ask for help from the union and are willing to accommodate many union concerns.

Values are also important in determining the appropriateness and degree of employee involvement. Ruh, Wallace and Frost (1973) have shown that management support for employee involvement was a key factor in retention of the Scanlon Plan. Conversely, Gilson and Lefcowitz (1957) demonstrated that a plantwide bonus program could fail because of a lack of employee interest in participative decisionmaking.

Organizational commitment is thought to lead to employee commitment and supervisory support for the cooperative effort. Employee commitment (discussed above) is a belief in the organization's goals and objectives, a willingness to exert considerable effort on behalf of the organization and a desire to remain with the organization.

Supervisory support is critical because supervisory resistance to organizational change as well as opposition to union and employee involvement have been well-documented (see, for example, Schlesinger 1982). Supervisory resistance is suggested to occur because (1) supervisors do not want to give up power and control; (2) supervisors do not believe workers are concerned about organizational performance needs; (3) supervisors do not believe that participation is an effective way to supervise; (4) supervisors do not trust the union not to take unfair advantage; (5) supervisors do not know how to manage under a new system and are not given adequate training; and (6) supervisors do not trust upper management's sincerity and support (Bushe 1983).

The transition from organizational commitment to employee commitment and supervisory support can be influenced by the strategy used to introduce the program and the effectiveness of future communications concerning the effort. This has been labeled the "acceptance strategy."

Employee commitment is influenced by the program's operational components. These are the availability of opportunities to participate in workplace decisions, guarantees of employment security, and an equitable and periodic distribution of benefits from the program. The operational components influence the perceived political security and member support felt by the union's leadership. Political security and member support moderate the relationship between union commitment and rank-and-file commitment. Where the union is seen as being instrumental to attaining program benefits (e.g., a bonus), and union leaders are not perceived as being co-opted, there will be higher levels of member support. The seriousness of the stimulus may also strengthen the political security of union leaders and provide more leverage and influence with members.

The model contains four general areas of program effectiveness. Program effectiveness is operationalized as improved productivity, stabilized or increased employment, an improved labor-management climate, and improvements in general organizational effectiveness criteria. The technology of the firm is believed to influence or moderate the degree to which employees can effect these performance indicators.

## Research Hypotheses

Not all of the elements in this model could be empirically tested. Research design considerations, sample size, participant cooperation, and the resources available to the project made testing of the full model unfeasible. Some issues were examined with a high degree of qualitative rigor, while three (organizational values, employee commitment and supervisory support) were not directly considered. They did, however, receive considerable support in many of the interviews that were conducted.

## The Impact of Union-Management Cooperation

Union-management programs were initially assessed along seven dimensions.[2] These were: (1) improved productivity; (2) stabilized employment; and (3) improved product quality. Reductions in (4) absenteeism, (5) turnover, (6) tardiness, and (7) grievance rates were also expected. This section outlines the hypotheses associated with this portion of the research along with a brief rationale. It should be noted that the study was longitudinal and all of the hypotheses were tested with at least 24 monthly observations prior to the program and 24 months following program inception. In fact, most of the time frames were considerably longer.

Hyp. (1) Firms with cooperative union-management programs will be significantly more productive during the 24-month period following the inception of the program as compared to the 24-month period prior to inception.

Kochan and Dyer (1976) have hypothesized that the development of union-management cooperation is contingent upon the presence of a strong stimulus for change. The academic and popular literature has highlighted the declining growth of productivity in the United States. Many of the firms studied in this research stated that productivity improvement was necessary for either immediate survival or to remain competitive. Most of the union leaders interviewed in this research also recognized the need to strengthen the economic effectiveness of their employers.

Previous research into the utilization and operation of numerous forms of union-management productivity programs has indicated that improvements in productivity are generally realized (Puckett 1958; Moore 1975). However nearly all the research in this area has been severely criticized due to defects in research design (Cummings and Molloy 1977; Heneman 1979), limited methods of analysis

(Heneman 1979; White 1979) and researcher bias (White 1979). Most of the reported studies have been case studies (Davenport 1950; Lesieur 1951; Tait 1952) using anecdotal evidence of program effectiveness. This research took a significant step forward in utilizing a time-series research design, unobtrusive measures of effectiveness, and more sophisticated analytical techniques. The primary productivity measure, output per hour, was considered a significant improvement over previous studies.

Hyp. (2) Firms with cooperative union-management programs will have a stable or improved employment experience during the period following the inception of the program when compared to the 24-month period prior to inception.

Employment or control over jobs for its members is a critical union goal (Perlman 1949; Thrasher 1976). It is no less important a concern for individual employees (Kochan, Lipsky & Dyer 1974). The economic survival of the firm and continuation of employment opportunities has traditionally been among the most common stimuli for union-management cooperation.

Improving the employment situation for its members is the critical outcome variable for the union. This is the case even when, as with gainsharing plans, there is the possibility of significantly increased earnings. A stable or improved employment experience is operationally defined as one in which the level of employment within the firm increases or remains the same over time.

Hyp. (3) Firms with cooperative union-management programs will improve the quality of their production during the 24-month period following the inception of the program as compared to the 24-month period prior to inception.

Hyp. (4) Firms with cooperative union-management programs will have lower rates of absenteeism during the 24-month period following the inception of the program as compared to the 24-month period prior to inception.

Hyp. (5) Firms with cooperative union-management programs will have lower turnover rates during the 24-month period following the inception of the program as compared to the 24-month period prior to inception.

Hyp. (6) Firms with cooperative union-management programs will have lower tardiness rates during the 24-month period following the inception of the program as compared to the 24-month period prior to inception.

Hyp. (7) Firms with cooperative union-management programs will have lower grievance rates during the 24-month period following inception of the program as compared to the 24-month period prior to inception.

It was noted earlier that cooperative union-management productivity programs are designed as structural and behavioral interventions. All forms of productivity programs in some manner change organizational structure in order to produce greater worker interest and involvement in the operation of the firm. Frost (1978) and Frost, Wakeley and Ruh (1974), and Katz and Kahn (1966) assert that Scanlon Plans result in a new form of organizational climate. Others have sought to describe the effects of these changes for Scanlon Plans (Shultz 1951; White 1979) and plans of a similar nature (Fein 1976) in terms of the individual employee's desire and ability to contribute to the organization. Steers (1977) and Steers and Porter (1979) have conceptualized this behavior as organizational commitment.

In addition, Macy and Mirvis (1976) include these variables in their proposed methodology for assessing the economic and behavioral effectiveness of innovative workplace programs.

Research conducted by Steers (1977) has found a relationship between organizational commitment and a series of employee work attitudes and behaviors. These included desire and intent to remain with the organization, attendance, quality of work and promotion readiness. Although the more macro nature of this research did not permit measurement of employee commitment, it did assess the impact of these change programs on the hypothesized measures of effectiveness. In some cases, since the hypothesized changes did occur, this now provides a further justification for research which would attempt to explain the causal process at an individual level of analysis similar to that conducted by Steers.

Finally, although it might be concluded that improved productivity and quality are conflicting goals, this is not the case even with the gainsharing programs. All of the gainsharing programs only reward employees for acceptable production, and because the costs of corrective actions are included in bonus calculations, there is an additional incentive to produce a quality product.

*Factors Influencing Cooperative Union-Management Program Success*

There are five variables included in this investigation as determinants of union-management productivity program effectiveness. Each of these determinants was identified from the research literature and was supported by qualitative evidence from an earlier phase of the study. These are guarantees of employment security; a structure for employee participation; the method, frequency, and amount of compensation provided by the program; an effective acceptance strategy; and an appropriate workplace technology. Once again, a limited justification for each is provided.

Hyp. (8) Firms with union-management programs that provide guarantees of employment security to the union and its members will be more effective than those which do not.

(8) (a)    The greater the degree of employment security guaranteed, the greater the effectiveness of the program.

(8) (b)    Cooperative programs which provide for employment security for union members will be more effective when the program and the commitment to guarantee jobs is made part of the collective bargaining agreement.

The expected outcome of a union-management productivity program is improved productivity and stabilization of employment within the firm. In spite of these desired outcomes, workers have historically been hesitant to participate in joint efforts. One cause of this resistance has been a fear on the part of workers that increased productivity will result in higher production standards or a reduction in the firm's labor force. In the other instances workers have simply not responded to the program. There is evidence which demonstrates the ability of workers to establish and enforce production norms (Roy 1952). In these situations the productivity plans have tended to fail. Guarantees of employment security also appear to significantly influence the success of Japanese management efforts to improve productivity and increase organizational effectiveness.

In order to overcome worker opposition, employers have agreed to employment security guarantees. These guarantees have included provisions for attrition clauses and no-layoff pledges, and have been effective in several instances (NCP-QWL 1977). Because of the legal nature of the labor-management arrangement in the United States, it is reasonable to assume that job security guarantees which have been included in the collective bargaining agreement will be more warmly received by union members than non-contractual guarantees.

Hyp. (9) Union-management programs that provide for formal opportunities for employee participation will be more effective than those which do not.

(9) (a)  The greater the degree of employee participation, the more effective the productivity program will be.

A number of different productivity programs contain various formats for employee participation. The nature of the structure for employee participation varies widely. Scanlon Plans and Quality Circles provide for formal systems of employee participation through an interlocking system of labor-management departmental committees (Frost, Wakeley & Ruh 1974). The responsibilities of these committees are subject to wide variation. Some committees attempt to generate suggestions from individual employees and assist in explaining program operations. Oftentimes the committees have the power to implement changes in their immediate jurisdiction (Cummings & Molloy 1977). These systems, therefore, offer individual employees the opportunity to exert considerably more influence and control over their work environment than would exist in more conventional firms. Rosenberg and Rosenstein (1980) have provided evidence that participation can positively influence productivity.

At the opposite extreme are programs which merely seek suggestions from individual employees which are then reviewed by management representatives. Other programs are nonparticipatory, that is, no direct effort is made to involve employees in the effort to improve productivity. These programs may not realize the full potential of the workforce or may be viewed as a gimmick by workers. This issue is an important one because there is some evidence that employee participation may be related to job satisfaction and satisfaction to performance (Katzell & Yankelovich 1975).

Hyp. (10)  Productivity programs which provide for group incentives will be more effective than those which reward the individual.

(10)  (a)  The greater the frequency of financial payments to the employees, the more effective the productivity program will be.

(10)  (b)  The larger the percentage financial payments to the employees, over and above regular earnings, the more effective the productivity programs will be.

Another feature of some union-management productivity programs is an incentive system based upon program experience (Lesieur 1958). If the programs produce improvements in productivity, a portion of the improvement in productivity is distributed to the employees. Kochan and Dyer (1976) have noted the importance of preserving organizational equity. The amount distributed to the employees varies according to the effectiveness of the program and the formula used to distribute the improvements (Cummings & Molloy 1977).

Reinforcement theorists argue that individual incentives are more effective than group incentives because they more closely tie the reinforcement to the desired behavior (in this case greater work effort) (Luthans & Kreitner 1975). At the same time, proponents of Scanlon-type plans insist that group incentives are more effective because of their ability to foster greater worker cooperation and the lessening of intrafirm competition (Katz & Kahn 1966).

Reinforcement theorists contend that the more valued the reinforcement (in this case the financial payout), the more effective it will be in producing the desired result (Luthans &

Kreitner 1975). It therefore follows that the amount of additional financial benefit paid to the employees as a result of the program should influence the level of employee interest, cooperation, and effort. The larger the financial benefit derived by the employees from the program, the more effective the program should be. However, reinforcement theorists also state that the more frequent the reinforcement, the more effective it will be in producing the desired result (Luthans & Kreitner 1975). There is a conflict. The more frequent the payout from the program, the smaller the amount of money paid out each time. This research provided some insights into that issue.

Hyp. (11)    Union-management programs will be more effective when the union and management develop a successful acceptance strategy.

(11)  (a)    A successful acceptance strategy will include an active program of training for first level supervision and union stewards.

(11)  (b)    A successful acceptance strategy will include the utilization of external consultants.

(11)  (c)    A successful acceptance strategy will include an effective communications program to keep organization members informed about the cooperative program.

Cooperative union-management programs involve significant organizational changes. In order to insure that change is successfully implemented, unions and management need to develop effective implementation and acceptance strategies.

The failure to develop an effective strategy will prevent rank-and-file and supervisory employees from becoming fully informed of the program's goals, operations, and benefits. Training for first level supervision and union stewards is necessary due to the significant structural changes which may take place at that level of the organization. When the program involves a bonus system, the use of external consultants can insure that both actual and perceived equity are maintained. In addition, both employees and supervisors will need to be kept informed of program developments and changes.

> Hyp. (12)  Union-management programs will have a greater impact on productivity where the technology of the firm is more labor intensive than where the technology is less labor intensive.

The technological process of the firm is seen as a critical aspect of the productivity improvement process. Most of labor-management productivity improvement programs are designed as behaviorally oriented experiments to induce greater work interest, cooperation, and effort. Successful programs should demonstrate measurable changes in the level of the firm's production. As indicated earlier, this has generally been the result. However, since most of the research in this area has not been comparative in nature, little is known of the compatability of particular productivity programs to specific technologies.

Research conducted by organizational theorists has found that successful firms in differing technologies have diverse structural forms (Woodward 1965). Labor-management change programs, and productivity programs in particular, should be viewed as changes in organizational structure. Therefore, following this theory that differing technologies require different organizational structures, a union-management productivity program should have an organizational structure that is appropriate for the technology of the firm.

A second factor is also relevant to this hypothesis. The more capital intensive or mechanized the firm's production process, the less impact increased worker efforts are likely to have. It is quite possible that where the level and method of production is nearly entirely machine set and operated, worker efforts will have little or no bearing upon production. In contrast, where the technology of the firm permits wider latitude of worker imputs, expanded employee interest, cooperation, and effort are likely to have a greater impact on productivity.

# NOTES

1. In this study it was not possible to collect individual attitudinal data to fully explore these models. A subsequent phase of the research is seeking to develop and test a conceptual model to explain the forces that influence employee work attitudes and behavior.

2. Three other effectiveness variables were later added. These included the frequency of productivity bonus payments, rater effectiveness, and program survival after two and five years.

# Chapter 3

# A Research Design for Evaluating Cooperative Union-Management Programs

Since the 1970s there has been an endless stream of articles, books, and speeches by academicians and practitioners exalting the benefits of union-management cooperation, productivity and quality of worklife projects, and other workplace innovations. With few exceptions (see for example Goodman 1979; Macy 1979) most of what has been said and written about cooperative efforts was not based upon empirical evaluations of these programs in the field. Instead, the historical approach to research on cooperation, the case study method, was maintained. In addition to suffering from all of the traditional difficulties associated with the case study method (see Campbell & Stanley 1963) the research suffered further from an absence of appropriate measures of effectiveness and analytical techniques, short time durations, and researcher bias (Heneman 1979; White 1979).

White, in attempting to explain the absence of empirical research on the Scanlon Plan, gave four explanations which would also be applicable to studies of other forms of cooperation. The low level of research activity, explained White, was due to (1) the difficulty and expense of doing research on organizations as the unit of analysis; (2) the inability to use sophisticated statistical techniques due to each organization being N = 1; (3) the inability to maintain strict research designs; and (4) the failure of the academic evaluation process to reward this type of work. Kochan's (1980) report to the Secretary of Labor earmarked change and cooperation as a labor-management relations research priority.

One objective of this research was to develop and refine strategies and techniques for evaluating the effectiveness of productivity and quality of worklife programs. This discussion will hopefully assist researchers and practitioners to assess similar programs as well as to examine the impact of other workplace interventions.

In this chapter, the research design employed in the project and some of the problems associated with it are discussed. This is followed by an examination of the methods used for selecting sites for participation in the study and the research strategy. Next is a discussion of the methods used to define and measure the key variables in the study, the techniques that were employed to analyze them, and the potential limitations of the research. The chapter concludes with a series of significant methodological findings.

## Research Design

This research was conducted as a field study which utilized a triangulation approach to assess the cooperative programs. Triangulation is the combination of several methodologies to study the same phenomenon (Jick 1979). Qualitative and quantitative evaluation procedures were employed. Donald Campbell (1979) has recently endorsed this approach to evaluation research.

The qualitative procedures included extensive structured and unstructured interviews with company and union personnel, examination and analysis of archival records and documents, and observations. The quantitative procedures included the measurement of plant performance (for example, productivity, employment, etc.); the scaling of the operational components of the interventions (for example, the structure for employee participation, the frequency of bonus payments, etc.); and union and management perceptions of the cooperative effort.

## Qualitative Data

The qualitative data collection served two purposes. The first was to permit a descriptive analysis of the interventions at each research site to be conducted with an emphasis on their structure and operation at the workplace. These data were later used for the comparative analysis of the six interventions contained in chapter 4. The second use of the qualitative data was to provide contextual meaning for the quantitative assessments and to identify other possible changes in organizational operations (for example, new machinery or plant personnel) that might have had a major impact on plant performance during the time period of this investigation. That is, the qualitative data were used as a check on the internal validity of the research design.

The questionnaires used in this research were adapted from the instruments used by Kochan, Dyer, and Lipsky (1977) in their study of safety committees. Other structured and unstructured items were developed to assess the process of union cooperation. Several models of organizational change in unionized settings guided this portion of the investigation. There were separate union and management questionnaires, but the instruments had many common items. Examples of the documents and records that were collected included the minutes of meetings, internal memorandum, suggestion logs, previous evaluations (internal or external), employee handbooks, and other materials associated with the interventions.

## Time-Series Designs

The assessment of plant performance was made by utilizing a stratified multiple-group-single-intervention-interrupted time-series design (Glass, Willson & Gottman 1975). An interrupted time-series design involves periodic measurement of an outcome variable both before and after a treatment effect or intervention is introduced. If the intervention has had an effect, it would be indicated by a discontinuity in the pattern of the data in the time-series (Campbell & Stanley 1963; Cook & Campbell 1976). Interrupted time-series designs are particularly appropriate for situations where the "measurement is unobtrusive and the respondents are not reacting to multiple testings" (Cook & Campbell 1976, p. 274). This research involved the measurement of output per hour, level of employment, voluntary turnover, etc., all of which are unobtrusive (Webb, Campbell, Schwartz, Sechrest & Grove 1981).

A stratified multiple-group-single-intervention time-series design has all the attributes of the interrupted time-series design. Its main difference lies in the use of multiple experimental units which are distinguished by some feature in those units. In this study the feature that distinguished the nature of the experimental unit was the type of union-management productivity program, that is, Scanlon, Rucker, and Improshare Plans, Labor-Management Committees, Quality Circles, and Quality of Worklife projects.

The strengths of a multiple-group-single-intervention design are two-fold. The design permits an examination of the pervasiveness of an intervention effect. In addition, Glass, Willson & Gottman (1975) suggest that it can lead to the development of a typology of units which react differently to an intervention. In this research the units remained largely the same, but the type of intervention differed. Thus the operation and effectiveness of six cooperative interventions could be assessed.

In addition, the basic design was strengthened in several significant ways. First, the measures (for example, output per hour and level of employment) were subject to frequent calibration into monthly intervals as opposed to quarterly or yearly time frames. Second, qualitative data were collected to determine whether other forces, outside of the intervention, influenced the impact of the cooperative program. Finally, by examining at least a four- to five-year time frame, cyclical variations could be taken into account.

## Sources of Invalidity
## in Time-Series Designs

There are several potential sources of invalidity in time-series designs. The principal one being historical events. *History* constitutes a potential threat when events that are extraneous to the intervention occur during the time in which the data are being observed, measured, and analyzed. These events may produce a shift of the series which can be mistaken as an intervention effect. In ex post facto time-series designs of the type used in this research "the danger of historical invalidity is usually quite high" (Glass, Willson & Gottman 1975, p. 54). In the present study changes in the economic environment were the principal historical events which could have affected the key dependent variables—productivity and employment. A comparison group developed from national data on employment and voluntary turnover (Bureau of Labor Statistics 1979) for three- and four-digit SIC industries was used to control for the influence of economic changes unrelated to the program. No comparable productivity data were available.

Other potential sources of invalidity that might have influenced the performance variables (productivity, employment, quality, turnover, attendance, etc.) or the change process were also addressed. *"Reactive" interventions* can occur when the system experiencing the intervention also undergoes other coincident changes. This is very likely to occur in complex social and economic institutions such as those under study here. Exhaustive historical analysis of possible confounding factors using qualitative data was conducted as part of table sites' case histories. Examples of systems changes associated with this research that might have had a greater impact on plant performance included:

(1) Substantial increases in capital investment;
(2) Shifts from production of goods with a higher labor content to products with less labor content;
(3) Changes in attendance control policies;
(4) Changes in key management personnel;
(5) Turnover of union leadership;
(6) Collective bargaining disputes.

*Multiple-intervention interference* can occur when the impact assessment involves more than one intervention. Thus one site which had labor-management committees later added a second intervention—organizational behavior modification. In another instance, a site with Quality Circles was scheduled to introduce a gainsharing mechanism. In these instances, the subsequent intervention must be considered part of the labor-management effort. In addition, computer software has recently become available which permits the dual effect to be modeled and each intervention component's impact can be assessed (Pack 1977).

*Instrumentation* constitutes a source of invalidity when there is a change in the method of observing or measuring the dependent variable during the time frame of the series. In studies using archival data, this is a problem when there are alterations in record-keeping procedures. Interview data were used to guard against this possibility.

*Construct validity* problems can occur when the operational definition of the causal agent in an experiment can be subjected to differing interpretations, thereby confounding the strength of the investigator's conclusions (Cook & Campbell 1979). In this research it was possible that improvements in productivity were not the result of the labor-management intervention but were simply the result of the greater attention given to employees by management, that is, a Hawthorne effect. This concern was minimized by the duration (at least two years) of the post-intervention time-series.

*External validity* can be threatened when there is doubt as to whether the results of an experiment can be generalized to other populations and settings beyond those involved in the particular research (Campbell & Stanley 1963). This study focused solely on manufacturing firms. However, it did cover a wide region of the United States and examined varied manufacturing settings. No effort is made to generalize the findings beyond the manufacturing sector.

Of greater concern was the issue of *self-selection* by sites participating in the research. Had only sites with successful interventions agreed to participate in this research, the generalizability of the study would have been suspect. It appears, however, that a cross-section of successful and unsuccessful programs was investigated.

## The Research Sites

### Site Selection

The acquisition of field research sites is never an easy task and this is particularly true in the labor-management setting. When the study began in 1978, the first 10 research sites with cooperative union-management productivity programs were selected from lists compiled in the *1977 and 1978 Directories of Labor-Management Committees* published by the National Center for Productivity and Quality of Working Life. However, publication of the Directory ceased with the 1978 publication and did not resume until the Department of

Labor began publishing a similar listing of companies and unions in 1982.

As the number of research sites grew, several strategies were employed to identify additional companies and unions. First, lists of companies that had utilized consulting services to develop cooperative union-management programs (Scanlon, Rucker, and Improshare) were acquired from the initial research sites. Second, the Buffalo Area Labor-Management Committee was asked to assist the project by providing the names and entry into three research sites. Third, participants at existing research sites were asked if they knew of other firms or unions engaged in cooperative experiments since these firms are frequently visited by others considering similar programs. Fourth, several unions with staff who maintain experts in cooperative programs were contacted. Finally, after the initial findings had been disseminated, several organizations contacted the investigator on their own initiative.

## Description of the Research Sites

This section contains a summary description of the major characteristics of the research sites. However, readers are cautioned that each site was given assurances that complete confidentiality would be maintained. The investigator has attempted to preserve the confidence entrusted to him by each site.

A total of 38 sites were visited and at least some data collected. Five of these sites were nonunion. As shown in Table 3-1 there is a very even distribution of gainsharing plans and Labor-Management Committees. Labor-Management Committees are categorized as serviced by an Area Labor-Management Committee or not serviced (i.e., functioning independently). There were two Quality Circles plans and one Profit-Sharing firm studied.

Table 3-1
Types of Interventions Studied

| Type of program | Number of sites | Number nonunion sites |
|---|---|---|
| Scanlon Plan | 9 | -- |
| Rucker Plan | 7 | 2 |
| Improshare | 8 | 1 |
| Other gainsharing | 2* | 2 |
| Labor-Management Committees serviced by A L-MC | 5** | -- |
| Labor-Management Committees not serviced by A L-MC | 4 | -- |
| Quality Circles | 2 | |
| Profit Sharing | 1 | |
| Total | 38 | 5 |

*One labor-management committee later added a gainsharing plan thus yielding an additional "other gainsharing" program.
**One labor-management committee experimented with a series of quality of worklife projects.

The study investigated organizations with eight international unions and one independent labor organization. Opportunities to study varied programs have existed. These include 9 Scanlon Plans, 7 Rucker Plans, 10 Improshare Plans, 9 Labor-Management Committees, 2 Quality Circles, and 1 profit-sharing plan. Table 3-1 summarizes the number and type of programs studied.

Table 3-2 summarizes six selected characteristics of the research sites including: product, SIC number, bargaining unit size, age distribution and sexual composition of the workforce, and the type of intervention.

All of the firms in the study are engaged in manufacturing, with a broad range of industries represented. Plants engaged in heavy industry from steel to tire production were studied as well as light assembly operations. Bargaining unit size ranges from 7-2300, with a mean of 620. There is also a wide

**Table 3-2**
**Selected Characteristics of Research Sites**

| Site | Product | SIC number | Bargaining unit size | Age distribution (percent) | | | Percentage female | Type of program |
|---|---|---|---|---|---|---|---|---|
| | | | | under 30 | 30-55 | over 55 | | |
| 1 | Fabricated steel | 331 | 1200 | 40 | 25 | 35 | 2.5 | Labor-Management Committee |
| 2 | Automotive components | 3694 | 500 | 10 | 70 | 20 | 20 | Labor-Management Committee |
| 3 | Ball bearings | 3562 | 699 | 10 | 40 | 50 | 22 | Labor-Management Committee |
| 4 | Jet engine parts | 3722 | 890 | 10 | 70 | 20 | 16 | Scanlon Plan |
| 5 | Steel chain | 3496 | 450 | 15 | 70 | 15 | 44 | Rucker Plan |
| 6 | Steel casters | 3429 | 129 | 40 | 40 | 20 | 44 | Scanlon Plan |
| 7 | Roller chain | 3566 | 241 | 20 | 40 | 40 | 44 | Rucker Plan |
| 8 | Abrasive cutting wheels | 3291 | 160 | 17 | 68 | 20 | 17 | Scanlon Plan |
| 9 | Steel shelves | 2542 | 150 | 47 | 35 | 23 | 0 | Scanlon Plan |
| 10 | Wire | 3496 | 250 | 45 | 47 | 8 | 1 | Labor-Management Committee |
| | Dropped from the study | | | | | | | |
| 12 | Gas compressors | 3563 | 250 | NA | NA | NA | NA | Improshare |
| 13 | Air compressors | 3563 | 95 | 18 | 60 | 22 | 8 | Improshare |
| 14 | Small compressors | 3563 | 20 | NA | NA | NA | NA | Improshare |
| 15 | Valve & regulators | 3494 | 23 | NA | NA | NA | NA | Improshare |
| 16 | Paper & plastic converting equipment | 3559 | 105 | 30 | 60 | 10 | 0 | Rucker Plan |
| 17 | Solid-state DC drives | 3674 | 15 | 40 | 60 | 0 | 75 | Rucker Plan |
| 18 | Electrical connectors | 3678 | 2300 | 50 | 27 | 23 | 35 | Quality Circles |
| 19 | Color television tubes | 3671 | 1000 | 36 | 42 | 22 | 42 | Quality Circles w/behavior modification |

| | | | | | | | |
|---|---|---|---|---|---|---|---|
| 20 | Dropped from the study | | | | | | |
| 21 | Food processing | 2032 | 1000 | 25 | 60 | 15 | 35 | Labor-Management Committee (A L-MC) |
| 22 | Industrial plastics | 282 | 1400 | 5 | 25 | 70 | 20 | Labor-Management Committee (A L-MC) |
| 23 | Rubber tires | 3011 | 796 | 19 | 71 | 10 | 1 | Labor-Management Committee (A L-MC) |
| 24 | Heat exchanger filters | 3443 | 85 | 25 | 40 | 35 | 0 | Labor-Management Committee (A L-MC) |
| 25 | Plastic injection molds | 3079 | 160 | 40 | 40 | 20 | 1 | Rucker Plan |
| 26 | Electric motors | 3621 | 200 | 0 | 70 | 30 | 33 | Rucker Plan |
| 27 | Cold forgings | 3462 | 123 | 40 | 40 | 20 | 10 | Rucker Plan |
| 28 | Automated assembly systems | 3549 | 370 | 15 | 70 | 15 | 10 | Scanlon Plan |
| 29 | Industrial fasteners | 3452 | 154 | 17 | 60 | 23 | 9 | Scanlon Plan |
| 30 | Nickel alloys | 3349 | 1530 | 16 | 63 | 11 | NA | Scanlon Plan |
| 31 | Sponge rubber | 3068 | 190 | 10 | 80 | 10 | 50 | Scanlon Plan |
| 32 | Heavy truck springs | 3799 | 109 | 0 | 85 | 15 | 0 | Scanlon Plan |
| 33 | Dropped from the study | | | | | | |
| 34 | Dropped from the study | | | | | | |
| 35 | Awaiting site visit | | | | | | |
| 36 | Lightbulb components* | 3696 | 174 | 2 | 75 | 23 | 50 | Other Gainsharing |
| 37 | Electric meter adaptors* | 3629 | 37 | 48 | 50 | 2 | 51 | Improshare |
| 38 | Portable car ramps* | 3549 | 27 | 85 | 10 | 5 | 40 | Improshare |
| 39 | Gray iron castings | 3321 | 240 | 70 | 29 | 1 | 15 | Improshare |
| 40 | Cement* | 3297 | 7 | 29 | 71 | 0 | 0 | Other Gainsharing |
| 41 | DC motors for material handling | 3620 | 170 | 10 | 30 | 60 | 31 | Improshare |
| 42 | Dropped from the study | | | | | | |
| 43 | Dropped from the study | | | | | | |
| 44 | Industrial fasteners | 3452 | 152 | 2 | 95 | 3 | 25 | Profit-Sharing |
| 45 | Insulated wire and cable | 3357 | 540 | 45 | 40 | 15 | 8 | Labor-Management Committee |

*Nonunion plant. Bargaining unit in nonunion plants refers to total number of production and maintenance employees.

range in the composition of the labor force studied. Some organizations have had no female workers, while several had 50 percent of their labor force being female.

Table 3-3 summarizes some additional characteristics of the research sites in this study. These include the state, community size, the type of ownership, and technology of the research sites. The sites are located in 11 states, they are in very small communities as well as in large metropolitan areas. Over half the sample was composed of plants which were subsidiaries of larger corporations (21), with the remainder about evenly divided between family-owned firms (8), and corporations (9). The plants had varied technologies ranging from fabrication of equipment in large stages to mass production operations. Two firms were dropped from the study when their level of involvement fell below a previously agreed upon minimum.

### *Control/Comparison Group*

One area where the project was not as successful as had been expected was in obtaining the cooperation of control or comparison firms. Sixty firms were matched to 20 of the experimental firms (three per site) from the Dun and Bradstreet directories based upon Standard Industrial Classification (SIC) numbers and firm size. These firms were contacted by mail with postage-free reply opportunities included with the letter of introduction. Over 80 percent of the firms did not reply, and only one firm that did reply was willing to participate in the study.

An alternate strategy was to use national data on employment and turnover from the Bureau of Labor Statistics publication, *Employment and Earnings.* In many respects this data provides a more accurate description of the historical events (particularly national economic activity) which the control group is designed to reflect. The issue of

**Table 3-3**
**Additional Characteristics of Research Sites**

| | Location | Community[1] population | Type of ownership | Technology |
|---|---|---|---|---|
| 001 | New York | 170,000 | Subsidiary | Production of large batches |
| 002 | New York | 35,000 | Subsidiary | Mass production |
| 003 | Connecticut | 16,000 | Subsidiary | Production of large batches |
| 004 | Pennsylvania | 53,000 | Subsidiary | Mass production |
| 005 | Massachusetts | 152,000 | Subsidiary | Production of large batches |
| 006 | Massachusetts | 4,000 | Subsidiary | Production of large batches |
| 007 | Massachusetts | 162,000 | Subsidiary | Production of large batches |
| 008 | Connecticut | 143,000 | Subsidiary | Production of large batches |
| 009 | Massachusetts | 63,000 | Family | Production of large batches |
| 010 | New York | 19,000 | Subsidiary | Production of large batches |
| 011 | Dropped from the study | | | |
| 012 | New York | 13,000 | Subsidiary | Fabrication of large equipment in stages |
| 013 | New York | 13,000 | Subsidiary | Production of large batches |
| 014 | New York | 13,000 | Subsidiary | Production of large batches |
| 015 | New York | 13,000 | Subsidiary | Production of small batches |
| 016 | New York | 13,000 | Family | Simple units to customer's requirements |
| 017 | New York | 13,000 | Family | |
| 018 | New York | 5,000 | Corporation | Production of small batches |
| 019 | New York | 7,000 | Subsidiary | Mass production |
| 020 | Dropped from the study | | | |
| 021 | New York | 2,000 | Corporation | Mass production |
| 022 | New York | 360,000 | Subsidiary | Production of large batches |
| 023 | New York | 360,000 | Family | Production of large batches |
| 024 | New York | 360,000 | Family | Fabrication of large equipment in stages |

(continued)

## Table 3-3 (continued)

| | Location | Community population[1] | Type of ownership | Technology |
|---|---|---|---|---|
| 025 | Ohio | 44,000 | Family | Fabrication of large equipment in stages |
| 026 | Ohio | 26,000 | Corporation | Production of small batches |
| 027 | Ohio | 1,000 | Subsidiary | Mass production |
| 028 | Wisconsin | 51,000 | Corporation | Simple units to customer's requirements |
| 029 | Illinois | 11,000 | Corporation | Production of small batches |
| 030 | West Virginia | 64,000 | Subsidiary | Production of large batches |
| 031 | West Virginia | 64,000 | Family | Simple units to customer's requirements |
| 032 | Pennsylvania | 12,000 | Corporation | Production of large batches |
| 033 | Dropped from the study | | | |
| 034 | Dropped from the study | | | |
| 035 | Awaiting site visit | | | |
| 036 | North Carolina | 32,000 | Subsidiary | Production of small batches |
| 037 | Michigan | 60,000 | Subsidiary | Simple units to customer's requirements |
| 038 | Wisconsin | 1,000 | Family | Production of large batches |
| 039 | New York | 5,000 | Subsidiary | Production of small batches |
| 040 | Massachusetts | 162,000 | Corporation | Production of large batches |
| 041 | New York | 170,000 | Subsidiary | Production of small batches |
| 042 | Dropped from the study | | | |
| 043 | Dropped from the study | | | |
| 044 | Pennsylvania | 10,000 | Corporation | Production of small batches |
| 045 | New York | 44,000 | Corporation | Production of large batches |

1. 1980 United States Census of Population, U.S. Department of Commerce, Bureau of the Census, Vol. 1 (April 1982).

control or comparison groups is discussed further in this chapter in the section on methodological findings.

## Research Strategy

In order to permit an intensive analysis of each organization, on-site visits were conducted. At each site, management representatives were interviewed and company records and documents gathered. At most of the sites, union representatives were also interviewed.[1] In several instances the fact that the site was nonunion was not apparent until the site was actually visited. On-site follow-up visits and extensive telephone conversations and mail correspondence were utilized to complete the data collection process.

The research was divided into two parts. First was an examination of the structure and process of change in unionized settings. This included the investigation of variables such as the stimulus for change, the internal political process to establish change, negotiation of goals, the structure of the intervention with particular emphasis on the role of employee participation, the method, frequency, and amount of employee compensation in the form of bonuses, guarantees of employment security, and the nature of the organization's acceptance strategy. These data were analyzed using descriptive statistics and correlational analysis.

The second part of the study was an analysis of the outcomes of union-management productivity programs. This included an examination of the dependent variables: productivity improvement, the level of employment, and the general organizational effectiveness criteria. These were analyzed using the interrupted time-series design.

An opportunity occurred during the course of the project to investigate five nonunion firms with gainsharing programs. By seizing this opportunity, it was possible to compare the unionized sector with the nonunion sector. These sites were approached in the same manner as the unionized firms.

## Methods of Measurement

This section describes the manner in which the critical variables were measured. It begins with a brief listing of the demographic variables and the method for their measurement. Following that are the measurements for the major study variables—productivity; employment; quality; absenteeism, turnover, tardiness, and grievances; employment security guarantees; the structure for employee participation; the method, frequency and amount of compensation; the acceptance strategy; and several additional structural and process variables.

### Demographic Variables

The demographic factors are noted as follows:

(1)  The type of industry was classified by using three- and four-digit numbers from the manual of Standard Industrial Classifications (SIC).

(2)  Bargaining unit size was chosen over firm size as being a measure more indicative of the audience the programs were designed to reach.

(3)  Program inception was measured from the date when the program became operational.

(4)  Technology was measured by using the scale developed by Woodward (1965). The instrument characterizes the system of production used by firms on a 10-level scale according to the degree of integration in the production process.

### Study Variable: Productivity

The measurement of productivity required a flexible approach. In this research several measures of productivity were utilized. The primary measure was employee output per hour. Two elements, labor input and amount of output, were necessary for the measurement of productivity (Greenberg 1973; Bureau of Labor Statistics 1976). Labor input was measured by employee hours worked, while output was measured by the quantity of units produced. Hence employee output per hour was measured on a monthly basis by

$$I = q_i \div l_i$$

where $I$ = employee output per hour

$q_i$ = quantity of output produced

$l_i$ = employee hours

Each firm was asked for this data as the most desirable method for measuring this variable. Approximately 60 percent of the sites were able to provide this information.

For a firm or plant with a diverse output, a meaningful measure of employee output per hour required a weighted hours index (Greenberg 1973). This is the most sophisticated method of productivity measurement, but was only available at one site. An alternative to this was to analyze separately each product line using the output per hour formula above.

One of the most significant findings of this research was the lack of sophistication by many firms in measuring productivity. In far too many cases, output per hour measures were not part of the organization's record keeping system. In several instances, this was due to the varied nature of the production process. In others, however, it appeared to represent a limited understanding of the concept of productivity. In these instances one of several measures was used:

$$\frac{\text{Deflated Sales/Production Value}}{\text{Actual Hours Worked}} \quad \text{or} \quad \frac{\text{Sales/Production Value}}{\text{Labor Costs}}$$

In the presentation of this data in chapter 6, the specific measure of productivity at each site is stated.

Finally, in the gainsharing plans, the calculation of the bonus represented another measure of productivity. This measure is particularly appropriate in the Improshare Plans, since the Improshare measurement utilizes some of the principles associated with the weighted hours index.

## Study Variable: Employment

The level of employment was measured by the average number of workers employed by the firm during the week of the 12th day of the month. Because employment tends to be influenced by prevailing economic conditions, the threat of historical invalidity had to be addressed. A comparison group of national employment data collected by the Bureau of Labor Statistics (1979) on an industrywide (matched at four-digit SIC) basis was formulated. At several sites employment was measured during the last week of the month.

## Study Variable: Quality

Quality was measured using the general formulas suggested by Macy and Mirvis (1976):

$$\frac{\text{Units Rejected}}{\text{Total Units Produced}} \quad \text{or} \quad \frac{\text{Scrap Dollars}}{\text{Production Value}}$$

In each instance this measure was adapted slightly to be consistent with the site's own measure of quality.

## Study Variables: Unexcused Absenteeism, Voluntary Turnover, Tardiness, and Grievances

Each of these variables was measured by the total number of occurrences each month, divided by average workforce size (Macy & Mirvis 1976). For example,

$$\text{Monthly Turnover Rate} = \frac{\Sigma \text{Turnover Incidents}}{\text{Average Workforce Size}}$$

Since turnover is also sensitive to national economic conditions, a comparison with national data, similar to the employment analysis, was conducted.

## Study Variable: Employment Security

Employment security was defined as the amount of assurance the firm has given to its workforce that no employees or jobs would be forfeited as a result of the productivity program. A two-level scale was used with "no assurances" and a "best efforts" contract clause at one extreme (low security) and a "contractual no loss of employment/guarantee of hours" or attrition clause (high security) at the other extreme. The collective bargaining agreements negotiated at each site were evaluated against criteria based upon contract clauses published in the BLS (1971) 1425 series, *Major Collective Bargaining Agreements: Layoff, Recall, and Work-Sharing Procedures.*

## Study Variable: Employee Participation

Employee participation was measured according to the structural mechanism provided for in the intervention for participation. Responses were departmental committees, plantwide committees, a plantwide suggestion system, and no structure for participation. In addition, collection and analysis of the minutes of meetings and suggestion logs provided some insights into the actual participation that occurred.

## Study Variables: Compensation Measures

The method of bonus payment (if any) in the intervention was categorized by individual, group, and plantwide payments. The frequency of incentive payments was classified into weekly, monthly, quarterly or annual periods. The size of the financial payout from the productivity program was classified either by the actual bonus paid or as a percentage of the bargaining unit's average hourly wage per employee. Another measure of compensation was the percentage of possible periods in which a bonus was actually paid. This measure was derived by the number of periods in which a bonus was paid divided by the number of periods in which it was calculated.

## Study Variable: Acceptance Strategy

The acceptance strategy was defined as the scope of techniques used to aid in implementation of the cooperative program. These included the use of consultants, supervisory and steward training, group process and skills-based training, and organizational communications activities. These variables were classified using a series of dichotomous questions requiring a positive or negative response as to their inclusion in the operation of the program. Open-ended questions were also posed to permit more complete analysis of these activities.

## Additional Study Variables

The stimulus for, and process leading to, labor-management cooperation and other variables associated with the design of the programs were assessed by posing a combination of open-ended and forced-choice inquiries to management representatives and union officials. A series of questions developed for use in this study was based upon the first, second, and third stages of the Kochan-Dyer (1976) model of organizational change in the context of union-management relations described in chapter 2. Other items were adapted from the questionnaire used by Kochan, Dyer, and Lipsky (1977) to assess the effectiveness of cooperative safety programs and from other change models described in chapter 2.

## Methods of Analysis

### Productivity, Employment, and Organizational Effectiveness

In this section, the manner in which the productivity, employment, and organizational effectiveness data were analyzed is briefly described. Readers interested in a detailed account of the time-series techniques used in this research are directed to Glass, Willson & Gottman (1975) and McCain and McCleary (1979). A more fundamental description may be found in Box and Jenkins (1970).

The interrupted time-series data were analyzed by fitting regression lines before and after the invocation of the programs (interventions) and then examining changes in the parameters (slope and intercept). Unfortunately, time-series data are not appropriate for ordinary least squares regression analysis. This is because ordinary least squares analysis requires the error terms to be independent. That is not the case with serial data which tends to be correlated.[2] Any observation in a time-series may be predicted to some degree by observations immediately preceding it or from previous random shocks (Glass, Willson & Gottman 1975). However, there are methods of compensating for this problem which eventually permit the data to be subjected to conventional least squares analysis. Those methods have been developed by Box and Jenkins (1970) and have been adapted for interrupted time-series analysis by Glass, Willson and Gottman. Their methods and computer software were utilized in this research.

The interpretation of the time-series data involved comparing the actual time-series for the postintervention data to what could have been expected or forecast from the preintervention observations. Thus a *change in level* would be interpreted as an immediate change in the performance indicator, while a *drift change* would be interpreted as a gradual shift in the time-series to a new level. Yet another possible occurrence is an abrupt level change, followed by a gradual decline in the drift. This indicates that the intervention had had an initial effect but was beginning to lose its potency.

In order to increase the sensitivity of the test, two features were stressed. These were the insistence that there be sufficient data points and that the data points be extended over a reasonable time frame. In this research, the data were plotted on a monthly basis, thereby generating at least 48 data points. This was considered to be within an acceptable range (Glass, Willson & Gottman 1975). The use of at least a four-year time frame—two years before and after program inception—should have permitted all possible patterns of variation to be accounted for.[3]

The statistical tables in chapter 6 include the error variance from the regression analysis and point estimates of the level and drift of the series at time $t = 0$ with associated t-statistics. The assessment of the impact of the interventions may be found in the point estimates of the change in the level and drift of the series following the intervention with appropriate t-statistics. In order to assist readers, some of the more interesting data sets are shown visually using computer graphics.

## Analysis of Other Study Variables

The thirty-three unionized sites were combined with the five nonunion sites to create a sample of 38. The relatively small sample size only permitted the use of descriptive statistics and correlational analysis. While the descriptive statistics and correlational analysis did not permit causal inferences to be drawn or the determination of the relative contribution of each of the independent variables, it did permit some tentative propositions to be drawn, as well as providing guidance for future research.

## Methodological Findings

As noted in the outset of this chapter, most of the previous research on union-management cooperation has been severely criticized. These criticisms have been based upon the almost exclusive use of case study methodologies, weak research design, absence of performance measures of effectiveness, poor analytical techniques, the failure to report unsuccessful cases, and researcher bias. Only a handful of studies have approached the subject matter in a scientific manner (see for example Goodman 1979; Kochan, Dyer & Lipsky 1977; Macy 1979; and White 1979).

One of the major goals of this study was to further develop and refine strategies for studying cooperation and change in unionized settings. The findings from this aspect of the study are presented and briefly explained in the concluding portion of this chapter on methodology. These observations are the result of the field work conducted during the study and ongoing monitoring of the cooperative union-management and quality of worklife literature. For additional discussion of these issues, readers are encouraged to see Schuster (1982).

### Finding: The Case Study
### Approach Will Continue

In spite of White's observations, wholesale defections from case study methodologies are not likely to occur. Quite the contrary, the case study approach will remain a primary approach to union-management cooperation research (see for example Drexler and Lawler 1977; Goodman 1979; Macy 1979). With some specific methodological refinements to enhance the scientific quality of this research, in-depth assessments of cooperative programs can add to our knowledge of the cooperative process.

## Finding: Industrial Relations Researchers
## Can Learn from the Program Evaluators

The generic study of change and intervention has long been a part of the discipline of program evaluation. Research on major forms of cooperative union-management efforts—gainsharing, labor-management committees, and QWL projects—could benefit from the research design and data collection techniques of evaluation researchers (e.g., Cook and Campbell 1976; Cook and Reichardt 1979).

## Finding: There is a Need
## for Longitudinal Studies

An increasing number of recent studies have been longitudinal, with time frames ranging from 6 months (Kochan, Dyer & Lipsky 1977) to 6 years (Macy 1979; Schuster 1984). This constitutes an improvement over previous work in the field, as long time frames are needed to assess cooperative experiments. Cook and Campbell (1976) have shown that organizational interventions may have a variety of different results over time.

In this study two plants utilizing Rucker Plans had abrupt increases in productivity following introduction of the intervention. In one case, however, the increase was followed by stabilization, while in the second case there was a significant decline. It was not until approximately 18 months into the Plan that these findings began to appear.

There tends to be a "life cycle" of events in union-management cooperation. Cooperation frequently begins as a result of stimulus variables existing in the environment of the relationship. It subsequently continues over time or dies out based upon the achievement of the parties' goals. Studies conducted over short time frames do not address the process and outcomes of cooperation when the newness and excitement of the "experiment" have worn off. Thus they catch only a small portion of the actual life cycle.

*Finding: Studies Should Utilize*
*Performance Measures*

Researchers should focus on the more significant outcomes of the cooperative process. There has been too much
research on attitudes toward cooperation and the
cooperative process in comparison to that which has examined performance. This is because many studies which attempt
to test these measures fail due to lack of cooperation by the
participants (Kochan, Dyer & Lipsky 1977; Schuster 1983).
The same problem occasionally occurred in this research.

Even when a research site is willing to cooperate and provide data, the experience gained in this study indicates that
this is only the first step toward measuring performance.
One important finding of this research was the generally
poor state of performance reporting sytems within firms.
Many firms do not utilize an actual measure of productivity,
that is, output per hour, but instead rely on financial
measures which often tend to be very sensitive to inflation,
price changes, and the costs of goods sold. Many firms also
have inadequate measures of quality.

Personnel reporting systems appear to be in equally poor
condition. Whether the organization maintained records of
overall attendance, grievances, and related personnel records
appears to be a function of the commitment of the personnel
manager, or in large companies corporate policy. Even the
plants of Fortune 500 firms were not found to have consistently good measures of either productivity or personnel.

In several situations, the method of record-keeping changed, making the data unusable for time-series analysis. There
were other instances where the firms provided data, but there
would be a year's data missing in the middle of the time
series. Once again, this made the data unusable.

## Finding: Studies Require
## Pre-Cooperation Measurement

Only a small number of studies (e.g., Goodman 1979; Schuster 1983), as well as this one, have examined "before and after" features of cooperative union-management programs. This procedure facilitates determination of whether the cooperative endeavor was having an effect. For performance, but not for attitudinal variables, this determination can be accomplished by using archival data.

## Finding: There is a Need for
## Control Group Research

One of the main ways of detecting threats to the internal validity of any experimental design is to observe whether the measured change of the experimental group may have also occurred in groups which have not received the experimental treatment. Thus, productivity may go up, accident rates decline, or employee attitudes improve for reasons entirely unrelated to the existence of the cooperative union-management endeavor.

At the present time, only two studies have used control groups (Driscoll 1982; Goodman 1979). This is probably due to the great difficulty of obtaining control sites since these locations have little to gain from their participation. It was a major difficulty in this study that was never surmounted and an alternate strategy was employed.

## Finding: There is Difficulty in Obtaining
## the Parties' Cooperation

Gaining initial entry poses problems due to the sensitivity of the cooperative process and, often, the inherent distrust of the investigator by both union and employer representatives. The parties tend to fear that a university academic (or his/her graduate students) will enter into the process and somehow provide a destabilizing influence. There is a fear that the researcher will inadvertently disrupt the process. This is compounded by the fact that, generally speaking, the development of cooperative interaction is a slow, time consuming, and frequently costly process. Hence, unions and employers may not want to risk upsetting their developing cooperative relationship to aid the researcher.

### Finding: The Values of the Investigator Must be Recognized

The personal values of the investigators involved in this line of research pose additional problems. Rosenthal (1966) has documented the importance of being cognizant of an experimenter effect which could influence research findings. White has catalogued the importance of research bias in Scanlon Plan research and writing. There tends to be presumption among researchers operating in this area that improving union-management attitudes is a desirable goal (Peterson and Tracy 1977). Another view, however, is that cooperation has worked more to the benefit of the employer and reduced union and employee effectiveness (Peterson, Leitko & Miles 1981).

### Finding: There is a Need to Study Unsuccessful Cases

There are very few studies of failure in union-management cooperation (e.g., Gilson and Lefcowitz 1957). This research actively sought cooperative labor-management experiments which did not succeed.

Little is known of the dynamics that result in failure. As will be demonstrated in subsequent chapters, significant data can be generated from investigating situations in which the cooperative process broke down. Unfortunately, investigating union-management relationships in which the cooperative process ended can frequently be more difficult than successful cases.

Unsuccessful cases are generally more difficult to locate. It is also more difficult to get the participants to discuss an experience that they often prefer be left to rest. There is no evidence as to what happens following the failure of the cooperative process. In addition, it would be important to catalogue the issues the parties confront following breakdown of the cooperative process.

# NOTES

1. At several sites the management objected to our interviewing union representatives. In several others, union representatives were willing to be interviewed but did not want to respond to the structured questionnaires.

2. The estimation of the parameters would not be adversely affected by least squares regression, but the standard deviations of the estimates would be. According to McCain and McCleary (1979), in social science time-series the bias in the standard deviation tends to be downward. Since the standard deviation is used in the denominator of the t-statistic test used to test for significance, the t-statistic would be inflated thereby increasing the likelihood of a Type I error (Cook and Campbell 1976).

3. Two of the sites had programs of longer duration and were evaluated on the basis of their continued effectiveness. The effective date of the last collective bargaining agreement was treated as the intervention point. This was done because in both cases the parties reaffirmed their commitment to the productivity through the contractual agreement. Either labor or management had an opportunity to end the program at that point. In these cases an analysis of the data with a three-month lag would have been logically unsound.

# Chapter 4

# A Comparative Analysis of the Structure of Cooperative Union-Management Interventions

This chapter of the book is a comparative analysis of the six union-management interventions—Scanlon Plans, Rucker Plans, Improshare Plans, Labor-Management Committees, Quality Circles, and Quality of Worklife Programs—which were studied.[1] Although the focus of this chapter is on change and interventions in unionized settings, most of the discussion would apply to the application of these interventions in nonunion situations. The chapter is descriptive and utilizes the qualitative data collected as part of the case analysis portion of the study, supplemented by other literature on the subject. This is believed to be the first time that all of these workplace programs have been comparatively analyzed. The goal has been to provide a descriptive analysis of these interventions primarily for use by policymakers and practitioners.

The chapter begins by briefly defining the scope of each intervention. This is followed by 10 topical sections in which the interventions are analyzed. Table 4-1 summarizes the analysis and reflects the organization of this chapter, which includes the following dimensions: (1) philosophy/theory of the interventions; (2) primary goals of the program; (3) sub-

## Table 4-1
## Comparative Analysis of Six Work Place Interventions

| Intervention | Philosophy/Theory | Primary goals | Subsidiary goals | Worker participation | Suggestion making |
|---|---|---|---|---|---|
| | | | **Program Dimension** | | |
| Gainsharing Scanlon: | Org-single unit; share improvements; people capable/willing to make suggestions, want to make ideas | Productivity improvement | Attitudes, communication, work behaviors, quality, cost reduction | Two levels of committees: screening (1) production (many) | Formal system |
| Rucker: | Primarily economic incentive; some reliance on employee participation | Productivity improvement | Attitudes, communication, work behaviors, quality, cost reductions | screening (1) production (1) (sometimes) | Formal system |
| Improshare: | Economic incentives, increase performance | Productivity improvement | Attitudes, work behaviors | Bonus committee | None |
| No Gainsharing Quality Circles: | People capable/ willing to offer ideas/make suggestions | Cost reduction, quality | Attitudes, communication, work behaviors, quality, productivity | screening (1) circles (many) | Context of committee |
| Labor-Management Committees: | Improve attitudes; trust | Improve labor-management relations, communications | Work behaviors, quality, productivity, cost reduction | Visitor, subcommittees (many) | None, informal |
| QWL Projects: | Improve working environment (physical, human, systems aspects) | Improve psychological well-being at work, increase job satisfaction | Attitudes, communications, work behaviors, quality, quality, productivity, cost reduction | Steering committees, ad hoc, to work on problem, informal | Possibly informal, depending on project |

**Table 4-1 (continued)**

| Intervention | Role of supervision | Role of management | Bonus formulas | Frequency of payout | Role of union | Impact on mgt. style |
|---|---|---|---|---|---|---|
| **Gainsharing** | | | | | | |
| Scanlon: | Chair, production committee | Direct participation in bonus committee assignments | $\dfrac{\text{Sales}}{\text{payroll}}$ | Monthly | Negotiated provisions, screening committee membership | Substantial |
| Rucker: | None | Idea coordinator, evaluate suggestions, committee assignments | $\dfrac{\text{Bargaining unit payroll}}{\text{Production value (sales-materials, supplies, services)}}$ | Monthly | Negotiated provisions, screening committee membership | Slight |
| Improshare: | None | None | $\dfrac{\text{Engineered Std.} \times \text{BPF}}{\text{Total hours worked}}$ | Weekly | Negotiated provisions | None |
| **No Gainsharing** | | | | | | |
| Quality Circles: | Circle leaders | Facilitator, evaluate proposed solutions | All savings/improvements retained by company | Not applicable | Tacit approval | Somewhat |
| Labor-Management Committees | None | Committee members | All savings/improvements retained by company | Not applicable | Active membership | Somewhat |
| QWL Projects: | No direct role | Steering committee membership | All savings/improvements retained by company | Not applicable | Negotiated provisions, steering committee membership | Substantial |

sidiary goals of the program; (4) structure for worker participation; (5) mechanism for employee suggestion-making; (6) role of supervision; (7) role of middle and higher management; (8) productivity-sharing formulas; (9) frequency of payout; (10) role of the union; and (11) impact on management style.

## Defining the Interventions

At the outset of this chapter it is important to define the scope of the cooperative union-management interventions. One caveat to this section is that in practice there is significant local variation in the design and implementation of each program. The presentation in this section may be considered the "generic" model. This discussion is preliminary to the in-depth discussion which follows.

The productivity or gainsharing plans (the terms are used synonymously) differ widely. Scanlon Plans involve an employee suggestion program, committee system, and bonus formula based upon the relationship between sales value and labor costs. Rucker Plans also have a suggestion program with a more limited committee system and a bonus formula based upon "value added" (sales value - cost of goods sold). Improshare Plans generally have no employee participation and their bonus formula is based upon engineering standards and total labor hours. It should be noted that Rucker and Improshare Plans are copyrighted programs. In practice, however, it is possible to copy the plans without the aid of the consultants. There are instances of companies and unions having done this, or where "locally developed" plans have incorporated Rucker and Improshare principles to fit particular circumstances.

The other three cooperative efforts, Labor-Management Committees, Quality Circles, and Quality of Worklife projects can be differentiated in several ways. Labor-Management Committees (L-MCs) are composed of the key management and union actors who meet periodically to discuss noncontractual issues, that is, issues not specifically addressed in the collective bargaining agreement. As these committees mature and a sufficient level of trust and confidence is achieved, the L-MC's activities may be expanded to include subcommittees involving rank-and-file members and managers at lower levels in the organization. In addition, the committees' agenda may be expanded to examine contractual issues. Quality Circles (QCs) involve shop-level worker committees that attempt to use statistical and problemsolving analysis to improve quality and productivity in their work areas.

Quality of Worklife (QWL) projects are more amorphous and varied and, therefore, more difficult to define. QWL interventions can range from cafeteria improvements and work rules changes to flexible work hours, autonomous work groups, and job redesign and restructuring. Some might argue that all of the interventions discussed in this chapter are QWL projects and that what is being labeled QWL is simply a collection of less utilized and publicized efforts. In this research, only autonomous work groups were actually investigated; the information on the other programs comes from the literature. Normally, L-MCs, QCs and QWL projects do not have gainsharing provisions, although there were instances in this research where gainsharing was added.

## Philosophy/Theory of the Interventions

In this section the terms philosophy/theory are used somewhat loosely. What is intended is the reasoning underlying the goals and structure of the interventions. In some cases, such as the Scanlon Plan, the philosophy/theory is better developed than in others, for example the Rucker Plans.

Of the three gainsharing plans, Scanlon Plans have received the most attention in the popular and academic literature. The philosophy of the Scanlon Plan is that the organization should function as a single unit, that workers are able and willing to contribute ideas and suggestions, and that improvement should be shared. The most well-developed discussion in this area has been by Frost, Wakeley, and Ruh (1974) who have stated that the Scanlon Plan is based upon organizational identity, participation, and equity.

Misconceptions exist when a firm attempts to partially apply Scanlon principles and structures. Several authors have indicated that it is the adoption of the Scanlon philsophy rather than a particular structure that is the crucial aspect of the program (Lesieur & Puckett 1968; Shultz 1951). Moreover, McGregor (1960) stated that the Plan was neither a formula, a program, nor a set of procedures, but was a "way of industrial life—a philosophy of management—which rests on theoretical assumptions entirely consistent with Theory Y." (p. 10) An organization's program is only a Scanlon Plan when there is an integration of the philosophy and structure into a package or system (Lesieur & Puckett 1968; Slichter, Healy & Livernash 1960) and only when the structure serves to implement the philosophy rather than the inverse.

Improshare Plans appear to have an entirely different philosophy. Although the originator of the Improshare Plan seems to support "consultative" management practices (Fein 1981), most of the Improshare Plans studied in this research did not have any shop floor participation. Improshare in practice is more a traditional incentive program organized on a plant or large group basis. Thus the philosophy of the Plan appears to be to tie economic rewards to performance, without any attempt at meaningful employee participation at the workplace.

Rucker Plans might be viewed as falling somewhere between the humanistic philosophy of Scanlon Plans and the economically rewarded and driven worker under Improshare. Thus, as will be seen, Rucker Plans have most of the same participatory elements of Scanlon, but in smaller doses or degrees. Managers unsure of the desired level of employee participation appropriate in their organization might select the Rucker philosophy as a midpoint.

The philosophy of Quality Circles closely resembles that of the Scanlon Plan. The premise of the QCs is that worker committees can solve production, cost, and quality problems when given proper training and support. As with Scanlon Plans, the QC approach is one of extensive employee involvement in order to produce commitment and identification with the organization. The major philosophical distinction between the QCs and the Scanlon Plan is the absence of a productivity gainsharing formula in the former. The QCs omit money as a potential motivator and rely on psychological rewards to drive the system.

The philosophy/theory of Labor-Management Committees is to improve the working relationship between the company and the union by focusing on attitudinal change. Once this state has been achieved, other significant organizational issues may be addressed and a meaningful discussion of long-standing traditional collective bargaining issues may occur.

The L-MC process is inherently slower than the process employed in productivity-sharing plans, QCs and some QWL projects. The latter three efforts accept the union-management relationship as it is and seek to implement immediate workplace changes. In all three instances, improved labor-management relations is an assumed by-product of these efforts. Yet the cause of the demise of so many productivity-sharing, QC, and QWL efforts is that they fail to adequately prepare both parties for the major changes that are about to be implemented. Frequently, adequate attention is not paid to improving the parties' relationship once the effort has been made operational. Worse yet are those instances in which management attempts to implement one of the change programs without involving the union.

In contrast, the initial goals of L-MCs are to produce a change in attitude between the union leadership and the management and between the workers and the management.

The focus is on problemsolving activities and building trust. The L-MC process exposes the parties' entire relationship, historical, present, and future, for review and analysis. Problems can then be identified and jointly developed alternative strategies considered. This process is the mechanism for building trust and confidence. Thus successful L-MCs permit the building of a solid foundation upon which further cooperative endeavors such as productivity-sharing plans, QCs, and QWL projects may be undertaken.

This is because of the central role that union-management relations play in determining employee commitment to the firm. For many years, it was believed that dual allegiance, that is, employee loyalty to the union as well as the company was feasible (Purcell 1954; Stagner 1954). However, recent research by Fukami and Larson (1982) demonstrates that the potential for dual allegiance is modified by employee perceptions of union-management relations. Therefore, if an L-MC is effective in improving union-management relations, it should eliminate the obstacles to employee loyalty to the firm, thereby paving the way for even greater levels of change.

Quality of Worklife (QWL) programs are based on the premise that improving the working environment will heighten workers' state of "psychological well-being" at work, and lead to increased job satisfaction. Increased job satisfaction will then result in positive work attitudes and behavior and increased performance. QWL projects can focus on all elements of the work environment—physical, human, and systems. Projects to improve the physical environment might include upgrading and humanizing the physical plant. The manner in which people are treated, supervisory style changes, work rules revisions, and the scheduling of work impact on the human aspects of the workplace. Finally, the structure of jobs, and the organization and flow of work are examples of systems changes.

It has been stated many times in the popular press, for example *Business Week* ("The New Industrial Relations,"

1981), that the management of the workplace is changing. These six interventions represent a change of philosophy by managers, union officials and employees. The six interventions converge on many key issues, for example, improving the psychological well-being of employees, increasing employee involvement, and sharing of organizational improvements.

## Primary Goals of the Program

Each of the interventions has a primary or overriding goal, plus numerous subsidiary goals. The primary goal of the three gainsharing plans is to improve the productivity of hourly employees, thus reducing labor costs. In contrast, the primary goals of Quality Circles are cost reduction and improved product quality. Labor-Management Committees seek to improve communications and union-management relations, while QWL projects seek to improve the psychological well-being of workers and increase job satisfaction.

## Subsidiary Goals of the Program

Scanlon, Rucker, and Improshare Plans share basically the same subsidiary goals. All three seek to improve employee attitudes and work behaviors (for example, attendance). The committee and suggestion systems of the Scanlon and Rucker Plans also seek to improve communications, achieve cost reductions, for example, in materials and supplies, and to make quality improvements. The opportunities for these latter improvements to occur under Improshare, absent the creation of similar structures for employee participation, is very limited.

The subsidiary goals of Quality Circles and L-MCs are to improve work behaviors, quality, and productivity. In addition, QCs seek to improve attitudes and communication which are higher priorities and more central to the philosophy and goals of L-MCs. L-MCs seek to reduce costs but, once again, this aspect of operation does not have the same priority as with Quality Circles. There is a long list of subsidiary goals for QWL projects including improved attitudes, communication, work behaviors, quality, productivity, and cost reduction. Additionally, and in varying degrees, most of the interventions also seek to achieve decentralized, flat and more humanistic organizations.

Most of the primary and subsidiary goals of the six interventions overlap when they are combined. Yet, important distinctions exist in focus and priorities. These differences lead to differential outcomes. Hence companies and unions seeking quick and sizable productivity increases would be best advised to use a gainsharing strategy rather than Quality Circles or a Labor-Management Committee. Conversely, L-MCs would be far more appropriate for improving labor-management relations than gainsharing, QCs, and QWL projects. Quality Circles are better suited for cost reduction efforts and are less likely to be successful in producing direct labor savings.

## Structure for Worker Participation and Mechanism for Suggestion-Making

One of the most interesting and important workplace developments of the 1970s was the increase in worker participation or involvement. With the exception of most Improshare Plans, the other five interventions in varying degrees provide for employee participation. Extensive employee participation is also possible with an Improshare Plan, although it does not seem to occur very often.

### Scanlon Plans

Scanlon Plans and Quality Circles provide for the most elaborate employee participation. Scanlon Plans have a two-tiered committee structure. Distributed throughout the organization (including clerical and office positions) at the operative level are Production Committees whose jurisdictions generally correspond to departmental and shift responsibilities. The functions of the Production Committees are to encourage idea development and to evaluate employee suggestions. Suggestions which are within a specified cost ($200-$500) can be implemented by the Production Committee as long as they do not affect the operations of other Production Committees. The Production Committees normally consist of two to five rank-and-file employees elected by their peers, plus supervisory-level managers. In some Scanlon Plans, Production Committee members can invite other employees to attend committee meetings. The Production Committees meet monthly on company time. The supervisor retains the right to veto Production Committee decisions, subject to employee appeal to the higher level Screening Committee.

The Screening Committee is composed of hourly representatives, the union leadership, and key persons in the management hierarchy. The Screening Committee has five primary responsibilities, including oversight of the operation of the Production Committees in three ways. First, suggestions which cross the boundaries of Production Committees or exceed the cost guidelines of a Production Committee must be approved by the Screening Committee. Second, as alluded to above, suggestions rejected by the Production Committees can be appealed to the Screening Committee. Third, it insures that issues or items raised by the Production or Screening Committees coming within the scope of the collective bargaining agreement, may not be discussed in those forums. Fourth, the Screening Committee considers current and future business problems, as well as other issues of organizational concern (for example, production difficulties and customer complaints). Fifth, the Screening Committee reviews the monthly bonus calculations.

## Quality Circles

Quality Circles normally consist of 5 to 12 employees from the same department or work area. The circle members are volunteers. The circle is coordinated by a leader, normally the supervisor who has been trained in statistical analysis, group dynamics, and problemsolving techniques. The circle leader attempts to develop the same skills in the circle members. Quality Circles meet periodically (weekly, bi-monthly, monthly) on company time.

The QC chooses projects they wish to work on. The circle then investigates the causes of the problems it has chosen and develops a solution to be presented and recommended to higher management officials. If the management officials approve the circle's recommendation, the circle implements the change and monitors the results.

In addition to the circles, most QC programs also have a Screening Committee to provide overall direction.

*Comparing Scanlon Committees and Quality Circles.* The Scanlon Production Committees and Quality Circles con-stitute a significantly different form of organizational struc-ture from that of more conventional organizations. First, in-teraction patterns among workers and between supervisors differ from conventional firms because the role of the worker is expanded. Greater emphasis is placed upon his/her ability to influence organization policy and improve organizational effectiveness. At many of the research sites, reports were given that "workers were listened to" for the first time. Second, in both programs, but to a greater degree in Scanlon Plans, authority to make decisions is brought downward to the same level at which decisions will be im-plemented. This is because Scanlon committees can imple-ment their ideas up to a certain cost limit. On the other hand, the QCs may get more management recognition because they must present their recommendations to higher management officials. When implementing ideas, the Scanlon committees and QCs are equivalent.

Quality Circles tend to restrict workers to focusing only on their immediate work area. In contrast, because of the Scanlon suggestion system and more highly developed Screening Committee, workers have an opportunity to influence a larger spectrum of organizational issues. Additionally, the use of a bonus formula, found in all Scanlon Plans but rarely seen with Quality Circles, tends to provide a greater focus on the total economic state of the firm. The statistical and problemsolving training provided to QC leaders and members is better developed than that found in most Scanlon Plans and may aid in making them more effective in determining the causes of organizational problems. Here again, there is a convergence in approach as some companies provided their Scanlon committees with "quality circles" training. At the same time, in many companies with Quality Circles, supervisors have authority to spend money, without further authorization, up to a specified limit ($200-$500), thus enabling ideas to be acted upon at that level of the organization. In these situations, there is very little difference between the Scanlon committees and Quality Circles.

Recently, several practitioners have suggested that Scanlon Plans are "the equivalent of Quality Circles with a bonus." This statement is only partially correct. From the point of view of structure and decentralized decisionmaking, the Scanlon Plan and "Quality Circles with a bonus" are potentially the same. In both cases, there are shop floor committees, a productivity-sharing bonus, and an effort to involve employees in decisions which affect them at the workplace.

There are, however, several subtle but sharp differences between the interventions. First, a Quality Circle tends to involve more employees (10-15) than do Scanlon Production Committees (3-5). Second, as will be discussed more fully below, the Scanlon bonus formula includes nearly all employees—production, office, managerial and professional. This is part of the Scanlon philosophy—the organization should function as a single unit. In practice, the Quality Circles interventions that have added productivity-sharing formulas have only applied them to the hourly or production workforce. Here the similarity breaks down.

In one Quality Circle's intervention, the circle's proposed solution was processed through the individual suggestion-award program and if meritorious, a group award is made to the circle members. This is very different from the Scanlon philosophy in which all improvements are shared by the entire complement of employees. In addition when a nonfinancial measure of productivity is used, the kinds of information typically shared with employees in Scanlon Plan firms is not made available.

Most important, organizations that have fully adopted the Scanlon ideology seem to exhibit a different set of attitudes and values from many of the firms with Quality Circles. Although difficult to establish empirically, managers in Quality Circles firms are more likely to maintain more traditional, authoritarian views on employee participation and involvement.

### Rucker Plans

Some Rucker plans have two committees, Production and Screening, while others have only the Screening Committee. In those instances where there are two committees, there is one Production Committee consisting of 10-15 hourly employees and an assortment of managers. The Production Committee meets monthly on company time and reviews the suggestion program and discusses production problems. The Production Committees tend to be used more for communication rather than problemsolving.

The Rucker Screening Committee is composed of the hourly representatives, the union leadership, and key management personnel. The primary purpose of the committee is to supervise the bonus program. In addition, production and long range economic issues may be discussed.

### Improshare Plans

The Improshare Plans studied did not have formal systems of employee participation. In some firms there is a Bonus

Committee to review the previous month's bonus calculations. Although the Improshare Plans that were studied had
no employee involvement similar to that of Scanlon or
Rucker Plans and Quality Circles, employee participation
would certainly be possible with an Improshare Plan.[2]

## Labor-Management Committees

Labor-Management Committees are composed of key
union and management officials who meet monthly to
discuss issues of mutual concern. The L-MCs may include
one to two rank-and-file employee members or may permit a
small number of employees to visit the committee and participate in its deliberation. The main body of the committee
tends to closely resemble the negotiating committees of the
employer and the union.

A mature L-MC program may be expanded to include a
series of subcommittees. In these instances, there will be a
greater level of employee participation. According to Robert
Ahern, executive director of the Buffalo-Erie County Labor-
Management Council (Ahern 1978) the general objectives of
in-plant L-MCs are:

(1) to provide for regular broad ranging contact and
    communications between the parties during contract
    term;
(2) to focus that contact and communication on positive
    problemsolving, achievement oriented activity;
(3) to build informal relationships, trust and understand-
    ing;
(4) to recognize the Union as a communication link with
    employee/members.

The initial goals of L-MCs are to produce a change in attitude between the union leadership and the management
and between the workers and the management. The focus is
on problemsolving activities and building trust. Thus the initial agenda items tend to be limited. A more mature L-MC
might be expanded to include the items listed below. The

degree of cooperation, trust, confidence, and the nature of organizational problems will define the actual agenda.

(1) Communication of business and operation progress and problems

(2) Planning for the introduction of new machinery

(3) Defining and publicizing quality problems

(4) Improving quality of workmanship and reducing rework

(5) Training for new hires

(6) Using production time and facilities most effectively

(7) Reducing equipment breakdown and delays in repair

(8) Skill training for employees and supervisors

(9) Organizing car pools

(10) Redesign of jobs in specific departments

(11) Definition and resolution of broad problems in contract administration

(12) Reducing absenteeism, tardiness and unnecessary idle time

(13) Developing alcoholism and drug rehabilitation programs

(14) Conserving energy and eliminating waste of materials, supplies and equipment

(15) Reducing unnecessary overtime

(16) Government mandated programs (OSHA, Affirmative Action)

(17) Improving cost performance

(18) Improving local health services

(19) Informing the community on company actions such as pollution control

(20) Productivity-Job Security Programs

(21) Gainsharing programs

(22) Cost reduction programs

(23) Security, safety, fund raising

(24) Sales support required.
(Ahern 1978)

## Quality of Worklife Projects

In QWL projects the nature of employee participation will vary according to the program. Some QWL projects will have no participation, while others might have informal participation or ad hoc committees to work on a particular project. Many QWL programs also have a Steering Committee to provide overall direction and policy. In the case of autonomous work groups, there is a high level of employee involvement because workers organize the manner in which the work is to be done, and who is going to do it. In contrast, flexible work hours and compressed work week programs might have no participation.

## Impact of an Existing
## Individual Suggestion Plan

Many of the firms in the study had pre-existing individual suggestion plans prior to the intervention. Under these plans, an employee who made a suggestion would have it evaluated by the appropriate manager(s). If the suggestion were accepted, the employee would receive a percentage of the first year's savings.

It is easy to see that programs such as this would conflict with most of the interventions. That would be particularly true of Scanlon Plans, Rucker Plans, and Quality Circles, and less so for Labor-Management Committees, some Quality of Worklife projects and nonparticipatory Improshare Plans. In the case of the former group, the most common solution was to terminate the individual suggestion plan. Although some employees claimed that they would no longer make suggestions, most employees did so in the belief that a bonus (Scanlon/Rucker) would follow. Moreover, most suggestion plans had functioned so poorly in the past—taking so long to respond to employees ideas, paying very small bonuses to employees, often paying a bonus for bad ideas to encourage continued employee interest, alienating some people whose ideas were rejected, and being very expensive to operate—that few people either among labor or management objected to the termination.

One Quality Circle program took an unusual approach. In that case, ideas emanating from the circles were treated as group suggestions, with the circle dividing the payout among its members. While this initially appears to be a feasible idea, not all employees who desired to be involved were in quality circles. There was a waiting list. Thus the unintended consequence of this action was to produce two groups of employees—circle members who were "haves," and noncircle members who were "have nots." In another instance, a Rucker Plan firm with a suggestion program that had initially been very active found it could, after two years, rejuvenate its suggestion program by giving a small gift for the "Suggestion of the Month."

## Role of Supervision

There is a dramatic change in the role of supervision with the implementation of Scanlon Plans, Quality Circles and some Quality of Worklife programs, for example, autonomous work groups. Supervisors chair the meetings of Scanlon Production Committees, serve in the role of circle leaders in Quality Circles, and assume a significantly larger managerial role in autonomous work groups (Goodman 1979). In contrast, supervision may have only a small role in the Rucker Plan (for example, serving as committee members and commenting on suggestions affecting their area), and Labor-Management Committees (occasionally attending meetings as a visitor), while in Improshare Plans and some Quality of Worklife projects, supervision has no direct role.

The Scanlon Production Committees are the key operating mechanism in the Plan and the supervisor's effectiveness is central to the success of the Production Committees. As chairperson of a Production Committee, the supervisor coordinates employee participation through his/her conduct of meetings and processing of ideas. Much of the firm's acceptance of the Scanlon philosophy and its attitude toward employee involvement will be expressed through the supervisor in this role.

Under the Scanlon ground rules, the supervisor maintains the discretion to veto ideas and suggestions emanating from the employees in his/her department and from the employee members of the Production Committees. Employees, however, can appeal the supervisor's rejection of an idea to the Screening Committee. This places the supervisor in a potentially vulnerable position as higher levels of plant management may overturn a supervisor's veto in Screening Committee deliberations. This possibility, once again, gives rise to a test of the firm's acceptance of the Plan's principles. If supervisory vetoes are never overturned, it is probably an indication that the Scanlon philosophy has not been fully accepted and implemented.

A final point is that in contrast to the other gainsharing plans, supervisors in the Scanlon Plan are direct participants in the bonus formula. This is part of the Scanlon philosophy that the organization works together as a single unit and shares the benefits from doing so. In the other two forms of gainsharing, Rucker and Improshare, supervisors are not normally participants in the productivity-sharing, but *may* receive bonuses through the employer's share of the improvement-sharing formula.

Supervisors normally act as circle leaders in Quality Circle programs. In this role, they organize the circles, train the employees to be circle members, and coordinate the circle meetings. Problems are selected, analyzed and recommendations made to higher levels of management. In order for supervisors to assume the role of circle leaders, they must be trained in group problemsolving, communication, and statistical analysis.

In autonomous work groups, workers take responsibility for assigning tasks, frequently with the coordination of the supervisor. The supervisor plays a critical role in coordinating the functioning of the group. However, the direct responsibility for supervising production is not present, as this has become a worker responsibility. The supervisor is responsible for planning operations and insuring that the work group operates effectively.

Quality Circles, Scanlon Plans, and autonomous work groups may be threatening to supervisors. First, the firm's expectation that supervisors can direct these programs by chairing Production Committees, through circle leadership, and group coordination may expose fundamental managerial incompetency at this level of the organization. Interview data at many sites strongly indicates that company criteria for supervisory selection and subsequent training and development are very weak. Therefore, it should come as no surprise when supervision does not successfully assume this larger role.

Other factors may negatively impact on supervision. For example, employee ideas and suggestions may expose supervisory inadequacies to higher levels of management (Helfgott 1962; McGregor 1960). Workers often become critical of management insisting that it become more efficient. In effectively operating programs, however, the supervisor's role can become more managerial. Rather than focusing on the control aspects of the position, the supervisor can spend more time in the planning and coordination of tasks.

In the Rucker Plan, supervisors may serve as management members of the Production Committee. Since this committee is primarily a vehicle for communication, the supervisor's role is very limited. In addition, employee suggestions which are processed by the Idea Coordinator may be channeled to an affected supervisor for comment.

In Labor-Management Committees, supervisors may be asked to attend meetings as visitors in order to expose them to the process and to keep them informed of deliberations. Because L-MCs provide a direct line of communication from the union leadership and rank-and-file employees to the chief operating officers of the plant or company, supervision and portions of middle management may be bypassed in the process. This also can be threatening to these groups as well. When, however, the L-MCs add subcommittees, supervision and middle management will likely become directly involved as subcommittee members.

In Improshare Plans and other forms of Quality of Worklife projects, supervision has no direct role in the operation of the program.

## The Role of Middle
## and Higher Management

Middle level and higher level management play a key role in all six interventions. These roles range from the monitoring of the bonus formulas, to committee members, and to evaluating ideas. In this section, rather than focusing on the interventions, the material is presented by managerial role.

### Calculation of the Bonus

In the three gainsharing plans, one or more managers are normally responsible for the assembly, preparation, and computation of the data necessary to calculate the bonus.

### Program Coordinator/Facilitator

In the gainsharing programs and QWL projects, one manager normally assumes overall responsibility for coordinating the program. In Quality Circles, this role is known as the *facilitator*. It is the responsibility of the QC facilitator to train the circle leaders and review the operation of the Quality Circles. In the gainsharing plans, this person normally attempts to maintain high levels of employee participation and involvement, along with responding to employee questions and concerns about the bonus formula.

## Committee Membership

Managers serve on the Screening Committees of Scanlon and Rucker Plans, Quality Circles, and Quality of Worklife projects as well as on the Improshare Incentive Bonus Committees. The role of managers is to give direction to the intervention and stimulate further efforts. In addition, the potential for employee communication is very great and many of the managers who were interviewed indicated that they used the Screening Committees as much as possible for this purpose.

Perhaps the most significant role for managers is in the Labor-Management Committee process. Here the full scope of the parties' relationship comes under scrutiny. The success of the L-MC process can be largely determined by the willingness of managers (as well as union leaders) to openly and candidly explore heretofore difficult issues. Through this format, companies and unions may address the need to change aspects of their contractual systems.

## Evaluation of Ideas

In the Rucker Plan, one manager acts as the *idea coordinator* for the processing of all suggestions. The *idea coordinator* directs suggestions to the appropriate managers for review and follows the idea through investigation to provide feedback to the employees.

In Quality Circles, employees formally present their ideas to higher levels of management for review and approval. This is designed to give the employees recognition for their efforts.

In the Scanlon Screening Committees, middle and upper level managers evaluate suggestions only when they exceed cost limitations, overlap the jurisdiction of several Production Committees, or are rejected by supervision. In the case of both Quality Circles and Scanlon Committees, managers may be called upon to provide information to a group working on a problem.

## Productivity-Sharing Formulas

The three gainsharing programs have elaborate and varied formulas for the calculation of productivity improvement. The Scanlon and Rucker formulas relate bonus earnings to financial performance, while Improshare is more a true measure of labor productivity. Scanlon Plans measure the relationship between sales value of production and total labor costs. Rucker Plans are based on the concept of production value (gross sales minus materials, supplies, and services) and its relationship to bargaining unit payroll. Improshare Plans are premised on the calculation of a base productivity factor involving engineered time standards and actual hours worked.

In the other three interventions there are no gainsharing provisions. All improvements, savings, and cost reductions are retained by the company, although they may be used to enlarge the "economic pie" in contract negotiations, thereby becoming part of distributive or wage bargaining. It should be noted, however, that it would be possible to implement the other interventions—Quality Circles, Labor-Management Committees, and Quality of Worklife projects—and later on or, presumably, simultaneously add gainsharing. In fact, three such instances arose during this research. In one instance, the intervention called for autonomous work groups, followed later by gainsharing. This strategy never came to fruition as the employees voted in opposition to the effort. The second intervention, which is presently operational, involved a Quality Circles program. Eighteen months following implementation, gainsharing had been added. In the third instance, an outgrowth of a Labor-Management Committee was the creation of a gainsharing program. Thus, gainsharing may exist independently or in conjunction with other efforts.

## The Scanlon Bonus Formula

The Scanlon bonus formula is based upon a relationship between labor costs and sales value of production. One common formula is:

$$\text{Base ratio} = \frac{(\text{Sales - returned goods} \pm \text{changes in inventory})}{(\text{Wages \& vacations \& insurance \& pensions})}$$

It is not uncommon to have the formula expanded to include other items over which workers have some influence and control, for example, materials and energy (Frost, Wakeley, and Ruh 1974). In these instances, it assumes an important element found in the Rucker formula. The great benefit of the Scanlon formula is that it can be easily understood by all members of an organization. A typical Scanlon accounting statement is presented in table 4-2.

At the end of each bonus period, actual costs are compared with what would have been expected using the base ratio. If the actual costs are less than expected costs, the difference constitutes a bonus pool. A portion of the pool is held in reserve to offset those months in which actual costs exceed expected costs. At the end of the year, however, the pool is distributed according to a prescribed formula.

The formula for the period distribution (usually monthly) and the annual closing out of the reserve account differ. The most common basis is a 75% - 25% employee/company split (Cummings & Molloy 1977). Less common are 50% - 50% and 100% - 0% divisions. The employee portion of the pool is distributed on a percentage basis, the base of which is determined by the amount of participating payroll during the period.

Table 4-2
Scanlon Plan Financial Data
January 1979
($000s)

| | | 2/12/79 |
|---|---|---|
| Gross Sales | $6,035 | |
| Less: Sales Return | (24) | |
| Net Sales | | $6,011 |
| Plus: Increase in Inventory | 566 | |
| Less: Allowance for Quantity Adjustment | (40) | |
| Net Inventory Change | | 526 |
| Sales Value of Production | | 6,537 |
| Allowed Payroll (30.97 of $6,537) | | 2,024 |
| Actual Payroll: | | |
| Factory | 1,452 | |
| Salary | 400 | |
| Total Payroll | | 1,852 |
| Bonus Pool | | 172 |
| Reserve for Deficit Months (25%) | | 43 |
| Bonus Balance | | 129 |
| Company Share (25%) | | 32 |
| Employee Share (75%) | | 97 |
| Bonus Paid as a Percent of Participating | | |
| Payroll ($97 ÷ $1638) | | 5.9 |

The Bonus Check will be Distributed
on February 15, 1979
Status of Reserve: January 31, 1979
Total Reserve      $198

The reserve is established in order to safeguard the company against any months with lower than normal output. At the end of the year (April 30, 1979), whatever is left in the reserve will be paid out with 75% going to the employees and 25% to the company.

## The Rucker Bonus Formula

The Rucker bonus formula is based on the relationship between production value and payroll costs of production workers. Production value is the difference between the selling price of firm's products and the cost of materials, supplies, and services. Once determined, production value and payroll costs are combined to provide a ratio. Thus,

Sales Value
- Defective Goods Returned
- Materials, Supplies, and Services (e.g., utilities)
_____
PRODUCTION VALUE

Then,

Bargaining Unit Payroll
_____
PRODUCTION VALUE

equals the "Plan Standard" by which improvements in productivity are measured. Table 4-3 shows the Rucker monthly calculation.

**Table 4-3**
**Rucker Plan Productivity-Sharing Results**
**February 1981**
**($000s)**

**Sales Value of Output**
(What we will receive from customers for products
this month.) $2,571

**LESS - Material and Supply Costs**
(The cost of the materials and supplies used in producing
that output.) 710

**Production Value**
(The value added to those materials in converting them into
our finished products.) 1,861

**Bargaining Unit Employees' Share of Production Value**
**at 37.74%**
(What the payroll would have been if performance
was no better or worse than in the Base Period.) 702

**Bargaining Unit Payroll**
(Actual payroll for the month, including a one-month share
of fringe costs.) 698

TOTAL ADDED EARNINGS or (DEFICIT) 4.3

1/3 to Balancing Account
(Used to offset deficit months.) 1.4

Cash Pay-Off 3.9

(continued)

The Rucker measurement of improvement is more sophisticated than the Scanlon formula. The Rucker formula not only encompasses labor costs, but also materials, supplies, and services and permits employees to share in savings from these items. The underlying premise is that it will motivate employees to be more conscientious in their use. Savings of materials, supplies, and services increases production value and the employees share in this savings in an amount equal to the Plan Standard (in the example above 37.74 percent). All savings in labor costs are allocated to the employees. Although improvements in employee use of materials and more careful utilization of resources can occur, spiraling costs of these factors of production adversely affected bonus earnings in at least two instances. On the other hand, several firms indicated that they felt that the Rucker formula was safer because it encompassed a greater number of factors.

#### Table 4-3 (continued)

#### Balancing Account
#### ($000s)

| | |
|---|---|
| Beginning of Month | 2.3 |
| Put in or (taken out) this month | 1.4 |
| End of Month | 3.7 |
| Eligible Hours | 52,136 |
| Cash Pay-Off Per Hour ($3900 ÷ 52136) | .075 cents |

Eligible Hours is based upon total straight time and overtime hours worked. The total Eligible Hours is divided into the total bonus to be paid, producing the hourly bonus rate, which two sites labeled the Cash Pay-Off Per Hour. The actual bonus received by each worker is determined by multiplying his/her number of hours worked by the cents per hour payout.

### The Improshare Bonus Formula

The Improshare Plan formula is based upon engineered time standards plus absorption of indirect hours and total actual hours worked. This concept is called the BASE PRO-DUCTIVITY FACTOR (BPF) and is calculated as:

$$BPF = \frac{\text{Total Actual Hours Worked}}{\text{Total Earned Standard Value Hours}}$$

$$\text{(Standard Value x Total Number of Units of Each Product)}$$

Example

$$BPF = \frac{500,000}{180,000} = 2.777$$

The time standard estimates per unit produced, multiplied by total pieces produced during the period yields the *Earned Standard Value Hours. Actual Hours Worked* includes all hours worked by production employees and nonproduction employees involved in shipping, receiving, maintenance and clerical operations.

Improshare productivity is calculated in the following manner:

$$\text{Improshare Productivity} = \frac{\text{Base Value Earned Hours}}{\text{Total Actual Hours Worked}}$$

which is same as

$$\frac{\text{Earned Standard Value Hours x BPF}}{\text{Total Actual Hours Worked}}$$

Example

$$\frac{4321 \times 2.777}{10,000} = \frac{12,000}{10,000} = 1.20 \text{ or } 120\%$$

Productivity Distribution

50-50 split

| | |
|---|---|
| Base Value Earned Hours | 12,000 |
| Total Actual Hours Worked | 10,000 |
| Hours Gained | 2,000 |
| Employee Share | 1,000 or 10% |

Productivity gains are represented by hours saved or gained and are distributed between employees and the company according to an established ratio, such as 50 percent sharing. The employees' bonus percentage is found by dividing total hours worked in the current period into man hours gained allocated to employees. Each employee receives a corresponding percentage increase in gross pay. Table 4-4 presents an example of Improshare bonus calculations.

### Table 4-4
### Improshare Productivity Calculations

| | |
|---|---|
| Earned Standard Value Hours | 2431 |
| Base Productivity Factor (1.48) | |
| Base Value Earned Hours (2431 x 1.48) | 3597 |
| Less Actual Hours Worked | 3279 |
| Hours Saved | 319 |
|    50% Employee Share 160 | |
| Hours Saved Actual Hours Worked | |
|    (160 - 3279) | |
| Improshare Bonus | 4.88% |

The Improshare measurement system has several advantages. First, it does not require the company to divulge proprietary information which might fall into the hands of a competitor or might be used to the union's advantage in wage bargaining. Second, the Improshare formula can be applied to smaller groups within the plant, rather than to an entire workforce. Third, in situations where there are shifts in the labor content of production, the Improshare method is a superior system for capturing these changes. Its primary drawback is that it is more difficult for workers and managers to fully comprehend and understand than are the Scanlon or Rucker measures.

## Produced or Shipped Dollars/Hours

The three gainsharing formulas are based upon an accounting of organizational production. An important issue is when the production is to be recognized.

Some firms credit production at the point of completion and placement into inventory, while others do so at the point of shipment to customers. Although this appears to be merely a technical issue, it has important organizational and psychological ramifications.

The optimal way to recognize production is at the point of completion. This ties the bonus, and in turn worker input, directly to the effort required at the point at which it was exerted. In this way the performance-reward contingency has its strongest bridge. Unfortunately, it is often very difficult or impossible for an organization to measure its productivity in this manner. In other instances, a product produced recognition system could be financially dysfunctional.

There are three important reasons why organizations cannot measure production at the time of performance. In small organizations, the information system is not sufficiently sophisticated to value changes in inventory each month. Recognition of production at the point of shipment is the easiest and frequently the only way to measure performance.

In other instances studied, the manufacturers of large equipment found that many products required a significantly longer production cycle than one month. Since these firms manufacture directly to customer order, they recognize production at the point of completion, which is generally the same as shipment. Sometimes, the large scale nature of the production requires a moving-average formula or a quarterly calculation and payout system. Recognition of production at the point of shipment is also necessitated when price fluctuations make the precise value of the production in doubt at the point of completion.

Financial considerations appear to play a major role in the decision of program designers to account for production at the point of shipment. This is a safer formula as the firm pays its employee bonus closer to point of receipt of payment for the product. In firms that experience periods where inventory is significantly increased, no bonus is paid until the inventory is shipped. In a recognition at point of production system, a bonus would be paid which could adversely affect the firm's cash position. Although not frequently recognized, this probably represents yet another hidden cost of building inventory.

Recognizing accomplishment at the point of shipment rather than production breaks the tie between performance and reward. Thus there have been instances where a large bonus was paid during a period in which production was low, worker efforts minimal, and even several where many workers were laid off. This can raise the spectre of bonus formula manipulation and can reduce employee understanding of the relationship between their efforts and organizational effectiveness.

### *Benefits from the Bonus Program*

Puckett (1958) has summarized the beneficial aspects that underlie the measurement and design of the Scanlon bonus system. Many of his ideas are applicable to Rucker, Improshare and other forms of gainsharing.

(1) The group bonus promotes cooperation rather than competition.
(2) The calculation of the ratio has educational implications for the organization; that is, it forces members to be aware of, and understand, key variables.
(3) Labor costs are a measure closer to work force controls.
(4) The standard is based upon the workforce's previous performance.
(5) There is a monthly payout, that is, results are provided as close as possible to when they are earned.
(6) The bonus is paid as a percentage of wages, that is, it approximates the contribution.
(7) The measurement process is a part of the productivity program. This opens up many dimensions for pro-

ductivity improvement besides working harder. It is used to communicate results and for generating further discussion.

Among the most important aspects of the bonus is the education of the workforce. In interviews with union officers and hourly workers, there was, in some firms, a greater understanding of the firms' economic position. However, the three formulas can be complex and some firms did a far better job of explaining to the workforce the operation and meaning of the performance indicators. The process of economic education is more fully addressed in chapter 6.

### Bonus Formula Manipulation

One of the most sensitive issues in gainsharing plans is the fairness and equity of the bonus formula. In unionized settings, all but two of the sites studied utilized external consultants to develop the bonus formula. This appears to be a preferred strategy since neutrality in the development of the bonus formula is essential. In nonunion settings, consultants are sometimes, but not universally, used.

Through the life of a gainsharing program, the need may arise for a revision of the bonus formula. This occurs when there is new technology or other changes, for example, when the price of materials or supplies rises sharply or quality changes occur. Improshare Plans provide for a one time buyout when the formula works too well to the employees' advantage. Although none of the Scanlon or Rucker sites studied had buyout provisions, presumably a similar strategy would be available.

It is more common in Scanlon and Rucker Plans to utilize the consultants on an annual basis to review the soundness of the bonus formula. If changes are required, they can be implemented by the consultants. If management and the employees/union are confident of the consultant's neutrality, this normally goes very smoothly.

## Frequency of Payout

Most Scanlon and Rucker Plans calculate and pay a bonus monthly, with a thirteenth payment being the end of the year distribution of the reserve. Improshare Plans normally calculate their bonuses monthly and payout weekly. There were, however, several sites which made their calculations weekly and paid a bonus on the same basis.

Some sites used a quarterly bonus calculation and distribution. This is done when the product production cycle is longer than one month, or where production or sales do not follow a relatively even flow throughout the year. Other sites used a weekly moving average formula with a monthly distribution system.

## Role of the Union

As the bargaining representative for the employees in all of these situations, the role of the union cannot be ignored. In each instance the union must either agree to the intervention formally, or at least give its tacit approval. Several firms attempted to implement programs (e.g., Quality Circles) without union approval, only to find an agitated union leadership working against employee support for the program.

The companies and unions in this study frequently included provisions for their intervention in the collective bargaining agreement. In other instances a similar result was reached through a memorandum of understanding between the parties. Informal union approval was given in at least two instances.

Union leaders serve on the Screening Committees of the Scanlon and Rucker Plans, and Quality of Worklife programs. In this role, the union leadership has a direct impact on decisions affecting the operation of the program. The union may aid in giving shape and direction to the effort and may provide support and encouragement to management to continue its efforts. In these settings the most important task for the union is to insure that the cooperative process does not invade the jurisdiction of the collective bargaining agreement and, in particular, the grievance procedure. Union leaders would also normally serve on an Improshare Bonus Committee, or if there were no committee, would at least be briefed on the operation of the bonus.

The most significant role for the union exists in the Labor-Management Committees. The focus of the L-MC intervention is on the attitudinal relationship between the key union actors and the key managers. The L-MC process exposes the parties' entire relationship, historical, present, and future, for review and analysis. The success of the L-MC process is determined by the degree of direct company and union commitment to the process. With gainsharing and QWL projects the union can be a passive observer. However, the L-MC process requires active participation and may require changes in union organization and leadership roles.

## Impact on Management Style

Scanlon Plans, Quality Circles, and some forms of Quality of Worklife projects require substantial changes in management style. Management must truly want employee participation and must be ready to listen to employee ideas and accept employee criticisms. The experience of many of the research sites studied indicates that once the process of employee participation begins, it is very difficult to return to the old style of traditional management.

Rucker Plans require only minimal changes in management style, while it is clear that Improshare fits very well into a traditional, authoritarian organization.

Labor-Management Committees require that management change its approach to union-management relations and its methods of operations. An effective L-MC process requires management to be open with the union in discussing problems, that it trust the union to be responsible in processing solutions, and that it be willing to listen to the union when it raises sensitive and embarrassing issues.

## Conclusions

Each of these interventions can produce positive results. The key factor is to find an intervention that is most appropriate for a particular organizational situation. Listed below are four issues of overriding importance.

1.  *What problems confront the organization?* Immediate improvements in productivity can sometimes be made with gainsharing. Quality improvements and cost reductions can be achieved with QCs, union-management relations can be positively affected by L-MCs, and QWL projects can improve job satisfaction and lead to longer term improvements in performance.

2.  *Which intervention best fits the state of the organization and the values of its members?* A poor labor relations environment is no place for a Scanlon Plan,[3] Quality Circles, or many QWL projects. Nor do these programs seem appropriate for an authoritarian management style. Ruh, Wallace, and Frost (1973) have shown that favorable management attitudes toward employee participation can influence the success of the Scanlon Plan. Do employees want greater involvement? Gilson and Lefcowitz (1957) have shown that lack of interest by employees can cause workplace involvement strategies to fail.

3.  *Is the management sufficiently competent to manage employee involvement?* Some managements are not sufficiently competent to evaluate employee ideas and suggestions. In other cases, management is too threatened to accept change.

4.  *Is the union leadership politically stable and secure? Does the leadership view cooperation as an avenue*

*for improving the well-being of the union's members?* A cooperative strategy can become a political issue in a union with an unstable leadership situation. The union's leaders must view cooperation as capable of producing results that could not otherwise be achieved through collective bargaining.

# NOTES

1. A major union-management intervention that was not part of this research in a substantial way was profit-sharing. It is hoped that this will be corrected in subsequent studies. Persons interested in profit-sharing should consider the work of B.L. Metzger (1981 and 1975).

2. There are reports of at least one or two companies with Improshare Plans that have highly developed structures for employee participation.

3. An exception to this might be where closing is imminent.

# Chapter 5

# The Process of Change and Cooperation in Unionized Settings

## Introduction

In this chapter the questionnaire data on the process leading to cooperation and union-management perceptions of cooperation are presented. Completed questionnaires were available from all of the management interviews (33) and from 19 union representatives. There were 18 usable matched questionnaires.[1] The five questionnaires from the nonunion sites were omitted from this portion of the analysis.

The theoretical models discussed in chapter 2 served to guide this segment of the research. In particular, the Kochan-Dyer model of organizational change in unionized settings and the Schuster model of labor-management productivity program effectiveness prompted many of the questions which were posed to union and management officials. This section examines the following process issues: (1) the stimulus for change; (2) the process leading up to the initial commitment to the change program; and (3) the operational issues in the design of the interventions. Following that discussion is a presentation of the perceptual data on the impact of the union-management programs. Tables 5-1

111

through 5-4 summarize the data. Each table contains both the union and management responses, with the union response in *parentheses.*

## The Stimulus for Change

An effort was made to identify and assess the factors that caused companies and unions to enter into cooperative strategies. Union and management respondents were posed a single open-ended question which asked them to rank order the three primary reasons for discussions leading to the cooperative labor-management program. These responses were later summarized into 16 categories. Table 5-1 demonstrates the wide variation in reasons for union and company participation in cooperative ventures. There were 13 different reasons given for company involvement, and 14 distinct explanations for union participation in cooperative programs.

Two major stimuli for company participation stand out: the need to improve productivity and the need to improve labor-management relations. Across all 33 firms the need to improve productivity was cited 26 times, while improving labor relations was indicated 16 times. Yet another common reason for the interventions was as a new compensation system (11 firms). Union participation in cooperative ventures appears to be motivated by a desire to improve wages (5 sites) and in recognition of the need to raise productivity (5 sites).

When the management responses for the need to improve productivity are combined with the responses of economic survival (5 responses) and foreign and domestic competition (6 responses), there is clear evidence that economic difficulties of the 1970s and 80s have forced a reassessment of company policy toward collaboration with their employees and unions. That 11 firms cited a need to improve labor-management relations as the most important stimulus for cooperation, 16 overall, highlights the growing recognition among managers that this aspect of their company's operations may have been neglected for too long. Since Labor-Management Committees, Scanlon Plans, and to a lesser extent the other interventions require active participation by the chief operating officers of the plant or company, these groups of managers appear willing to commit themselves to working with employees and unions toward improvements in labor-management relations and increased organizational effectiveness.

Table 5-1
Management and Union Responses
to the Stimulus for Change and Cooperation

| Stimulus | Rank Order | | | |
|---|---|---|---|---|
| | 1 | 2 | 3 | Total |
| Economic Survival | 3 | 1 | 1 | 5 |
| Improve Productivity | 6 | 17 (5) | 3 | 26 (5) |
| For/Dom Competition | 3 | 1 (1) | 2 | 6 (1) |
| Corporate Pressure | -- | -- | 2 | 2 |
| Improve L-M Relations | 11 (2) | -- (1) | 5 (1) | 16 (4) |
| Improve Communications | 2 | 2 | 3 (2) | 7 (2) |
| Motivational Technique | 1 (1) | 2 (1) | 3 | 6 (2) |
| Problemsolving Technique | -- | -- (2) | 2 (1) | 2 (3) |
| New Compensation System | 2 (3) | 7 | 2 | 11 (3) |
| Improve Wages | 4 (7) | 1 | -- | 5 (7) |
| Reduce Turnover | -- | -- | 1 | 1 |
| Company Proposal | -- (1) | -- (1) | -- | -- (2) |
| Job Security | -- (2) | -- (2) | -- | -- (3) |
| Improve Working Conditions | -- (1) | -- | -- (2) | -- (3) |
| Improve Quality | 1 (1) | -- | 1 | 2 (1) |
| Improve Relationship Between Direct/Indirect Employees | -- | -- | 1 (4) | 1 (4) |
| No response/NA | 0 (15) | 2 (20) | 7 (23) | |

The number of managers who cited as a stimulus the need to develop a new compensation (incentive) system raises a note of concern. An observation from this research, supported by several interviewees, was that too many companies rely on incentive programs to manage employee work efforts, rather than on competent supervision. More important, overemphasis on the incentive aspects of the gainsharing plans is contrary to the full thrust of these programs. The participation, involvement, sharing of ideas and information, and building of trust in the organization, all integral aspects of gainsharing plans, may not be fully realized when the primary reason for the change is to replace an out-of-date incentive system or to create one where none existed before.

Several union respondents failed to fully answer this question, but of those who did, a sizable proportion saw improving wages (7 responses) as the stimulus to enter into the cooperative program. A sizable proportion of union respondents (5 responses) also recognized the need to improve productivity.

Thus both from the management and labor point of view, the stimulus for change and cooperation is based almost exclusively upon pragmatic concerns, such as the need to improve productivity, increase wages, strengthen the economic well-being of the company, improve labor-management relations, address payment systems difficulties, and solve other organizational problems. There was no discussion in any of the interviews of the need to increase worker control or to give cooperation and change of a more political emphasis, as might be found in Western Europe. The stimulus for American union-management cooperation and employee participation is entirely consistent with the ideology of the American industrial relations system. Cooperation is based upon a series of pragmatic responses to environmental problems impacting upon the employment relationship.

## The Process of Change

Table 5-2 presents the management and union responses to a series of forced-choice questions related to the process of change. Open-ended questions were used to supplement this analysis. The questions focused on: (1) whether efforts had been made to resolve the stimulus issues in collective bargaining; (2) the existence of coalitions to block the programs; (3) the use of neutrals and consultants; and (4) the degree to which the program was viewed as instrumental in resolving the stimulus issues.

The limited data in table 5-2 substantiate several theoretical propositions concerning union-management change and cooperation. Seventy-three percent of the management and 72 percent of the union respondents indicated that they had unsuccessfully attempted to resolve the stimulus issues in collective bargaining. Thus, as predicted in the Kochan-Dyer model, change in union-management settings is only likely to occur when the parties' traditional method of interaction (collective bargaining) is ineffective in resolving the stimulus issues. This finding has important practical and policy implications.

The existence of political opposition to a change program was also suggested by Kochan and Dyer as an obstacle to implementation. As expected, the data in table 5-2 show this to be a more significant problem for the union (33 percent) than for management (19 percent). Companies will need to be sensitive to internal union politics when collaborating on change programs.

Political pressures within the union can pose serious difficulties for even the most secure union leadership. Although this opposition oftentimes only represents a vocal minority, it can constrict the maneuverability of the leadership. Opposition coalitions are a potential obstacle to cooperation in both the initial stages of discussion and once the cooperative program has been implemented.

### Table 5-2
### Management and Union Responses
### to the Process of Change

|  | Yes | No | NA |
|---|---|---|---|
| Resolution via Collective Bargaining | 24 (13) | 8 (5) | 1 (15) |
| Percent | 73 (72) | 24 (28) | 3 |
| Opposition Coalitions | 6 (6) | 24 (12) | 2 (15) |
| Percent | 19 (33) | 75 (66) | 6 |
| Use of Neutrals/Consultants[a] | 28 | 4 | 1 |
| Percent | 88 | 13 |  |
|  | **Frequency** | **Percent** |  |
| Instrumentality of the Program |  |  |  |
| not very useful | 1 (1) | 3 (5) |  |
| questioned usefulness | 1 (5) | 3 (26) |  |
| might have been useful | 1 (2) | 3 (11) |  |
| somewhat useful | 10 (6) | 31 (32) |  |
| very useful | 19 (5) | 59 (26) |  |

a. Includes only management responses.

In the sample of relationships studied, several ways were used to reduce the likelihood of this occurring. First, realistic understandings of what the cooperative process meant were achieved at the outset. This can defuse the initial assumption that the leadership has been co-opted or has sold out to management. Second, vocal skeptics were brought into the process as visiting attendees at meetings or by giving them committee responsibilities. Third, union members were kept informed through the posting of committee minutes and other union and company communications efforts. Fourth, and most important of all, management representatives were sensitive to this problem and in several instances avoided creating situations which might compromise the union leadership. Finally, some union leaders chose to play an oversight role rather than direct role in the operation of the program.

A very common problem is the lack of skill possessed by the parties in devising and implementing cooperative strategies. Several theoretical models suggest the necessity for qualified consultants. There is presently no shortage of consultants available to assist the parties. However, many of these consultants are not qualified to work in unionized settings. There are inherent differences between union and nonunion settings which must be recognized when devising change strategies. There appears to be a limited supply of neutrals and consultants who possess both a wide array of behavioral science training and a thorough background in the mechanics and implications of the collective bargaining agreement.

The data in table 5-2 show that in 88 percent of the interventions neutrals or consultants were utilized. In most cases the consultants appeared reasonably well-qualified in the labor relations area. In one instance involving a Labor-Management Committee which eventually recommended an elaborate Quality of Worklife program, interview data strongly suggested that the consultants did not fully understand the labor relations environment. In this instance the intervention failed. The Labor-Management Committees which were guided by the expertise of an Area Labor-Management Committee appeared to be more effective than those L-MCs which operated independently.

The item measuring instrumentality produced one of the most interesting findings. It is apparent that union leaders do not perceive labor-management cooperation efforts as being as likely to succeed as their management counterparts. Only 26 percent of the union leaders viewed the effort as being "very useful," as compared to 59 percent for the management respondents. Thirty-one percent of the union representatives were skeptical of the intervention as compared to only 6 percent for the management respondents. Perhaps the management respondents believed that their organization and careers could derive greater benefits from cooperation than did their union counterparts. Moreover, since most change programs were first proposed by the company, management representatives would be more likely to view the effort as having a greater potential in solving organizational problems. Union leaders, being on the receiving end of a long stream of management proposals to improve an assortment of employee and performance difficulties would be more likely to be skeptical.

## Operational Issues

The focus of this section is on the relationship between the intervention and the grievance procedure, guarantees of employment security, and opportunities for employee participation, changes in training programs, and the structure of the bonus sharing formula. Table 5-3 presents the management responses to the questionnaire items on the structural aspects of the change program. Only the management responses have been used because they constitute the larger sample and the data provided could be verified by other documents and records. On the gainsharing and training variables, the union sample was combined with the nonunion sample to equal 38 sites. Once again, there are several interesting and important findings.

The theoretical (Kochan and Dyer 1976) and conventional (Ahern 1978) wisdom has been that the cooperative process should be kept separate from the negotiations process and grievance procedure. This principle is frequently raised as a means of reducing resistance to initial participation in a cooperative venture. Seventy-three percent of the cooperative efforts prohibit the program from overlapping the grievance procedure. This is considered an important element in maintaining the proper relationship between the traditional collective bargaining process and the cooperative endeavor. However, at eight sites, the program did overlap the grievance procedure. As a practical matter, the cooperative process can only be kept separate from the negotiations and grievance procedures when the parties are addressing relatively minor problems. As the parties begin to discuss significant issues affecting their relationship, they will oftentimes find that it is difficult to achieve and maintain this separation, as the cooperative and traditional processes are frequently intertwined. An example of this would be the case of the Labor-Management Committee which examined the issue of limited promotion and job mobility opportunities within the bargaining unit—a meaningful and appropriate issue for the cooperative process. Because parties' collective bargaining agreement clearly specified both manning and job assignment rules, a potential conflict was thus created. The critical issue in these cases is how to maintain the integrity of the traditional process, while at the same time utilizing the cooperative process to the fullest extent. Three distinct problem areas were identified.

**Table 5-3**
**Design of Union-Management Interventions**

| | Yes | No | NA |
|---|---|---|---|
| Overlap Grievance Procedure | 8 | 24 | 1 |
| Percent | 24 | 73 | 3 |
| Job Security Guarantees | 3 | 29 | 1 |
| Percent | 9 | 88 | 3 |
| Job Guarantees in Contract | 2 | 1 | 30 |
| Percent | 67 | 33 | |
| Employee Participation | 27 | 5 | 1 |
| Percent | 81 | 15 | 3 |
| Training Supervisors/Stewards | 20 | 13 | |
| Percent | 61 | 39 | |
| Changed Skill Training[a] | 10 | 24 | 4 |
| Percent | 29 | 71 | |
| Bonus Sharing Program[a] | 28 | 10 | |
| Percent | 74 | 26 | |

| | Frequency | Percentage |
|---|---|---|
| Basis of Bonus Distribution[a] | | |
| Group | 9 | 32 |
| Plantwide | 19 | 68 |
| Other/NA | 10 | |
| Frequency of Bonus Distribution[a] | | |
| Weekly | 9 | 33 |
| Monthly | 14 | 52 |
| Quarterly | 4 | 15 |
| Other/NA | 11 | |

a. Includes both union and nonunion firms.

The first problem area arises when a matter that is the subject of an active grievance is raised in the cooperative process. An often-used strategy is for an active grievance to be treated as solely within the jurisdiction of the grievance procedure, whereas issues which cause or have caused grievances are appropriate issues for the cooperative process.

A second problem area occurs when change, particularly meaningful change, requires modification of, or additions to, the collective bargaining agreement. This occurs when the participants to the cooperative process determine that their relationship would be best served by incorporating their accomplishments into the "web of rules" of the collective agreement. A question often arises as to when and how this is to be accomplished. In some instances, a memorandum of understanding is executed and appended to an existing agreement. In other cases, however, the parties delay change until the next round of negotiations and incorporate it into a new agreement.

The third problem area is whether the cooperative process should be suspended during negotiations. The fear expressed in these situations is that aggressive tactics at the bargaining table in the pursuit of distributive goals will upset the tentative trust and good faith established in the cooperative process. No clear solution has emerged, and situations could be found where either strategy has been successful. There is no doubt, however, that when the cooperative process is effective, it reduces the conflict inherent in the traditional collective bargaining process.

Although a great deal has been written about Japanese management systems and their provisions for guaranteed employment, the presence of meaningful job security guarantees on the American labor relations scene has yet to occur. Just three (9 percent) of the firms provided any form of employment security guarantees. Of these, one was a preexisting supplemental unemployment benefits plan, another was a "best efforts to maintain employment" provision, and in only one case was there a contract clause providing for "no loss of employment" as a result of the intervention. Twenty-eight sites (88 percent) had no provision for employment security. It should be noted, however, that job security was an often discussed issue by both union and management respondents. Yet, there does not seem to be very much interest in attempting to institutionalize job protections.

One of the most dramatic changes taking place in the American industrial relations system is the increase in employee participation at the workplace ("The New Industrial Relations" 1981). In this research, 27 (84 percent) firms provided for some structure for employee involvement. Although this is only a general finding, it does indicate that a significant shift is taking place in management and union attitudes about the proper role for employee participation. Through the qualitative data collection, other questions such as the amount and quality of employee participation were addressed. Some of these findings will be discussed in the next chapter.

As was discussed in chapter 3 several of the interventions require changes in management style and an expanded role for the union. It would be expected that these changes could not be instituted without properly preparing the organization. At 20 firms (61 percent), training programs for supervisors and/or union stewards were part of the institution and maintenance of the change effort.

In addition, as employee involvement increased, employee skill training requirements were found to change. Two primary reasons surfaced in the qualitative data collected. First, employee involvement permitted workers to bring to the attention of company decisionmakers the need for additional training to adequately perform existing jobs. Second, one result of employee involvement at several sites was an expression of worker interest in job restructuring. For example, at least one firm added inspection functions to production jobs which necessitated training on computer measurement machinery.

To examine the gainsharing aspects of the interventions, the nonunion sample was combined with the union sample. Twenty-nine (74 percent) of the 38 sites had a bonus sharing program. Of these, 18 (67 percent) paid a bonus on a plantwide basis and 9 (33 percent) on a group bonus system. Over half the gainsharing plans (14 sites) paid a bonus on a monthly basis, while nine paid a weekly bonus, and four paid quarterly.

## Perceptions of the Impact of Change

Effective union-management cooperation should have a positive impact on labor-management relations and on the process of improving productivity. Respondents were given an eight-item, forced-choice instrument which asked: "To what extent do you agree or disagree with each of the following statements relating to union involvement on productivity issues?" Four other items dealt with perceptions of hostility and cooperation in the overall union-management relationship, on the specific issue of productivity, on top management commitment to productivity improvement, and on the role the union should play in the area of plant productivity improvement. The results are provided in table 5-4. Once again union responses are in parentheses.

The responses to Item 9 seemed to indicate that company and union respondents believed their relationships were somewhat to very cooperative (81 percent for management, 83 percent for the union). More important, the parties agreed on the state of their relationship, as the correlation between management and union responses was .62 (p < .01). Similarly, the respondents seemed to believe that there was a good deal of cooperation on the specific issue of productivity. Seventy-three percent of the management respondents

**Table 5-4**
**Management and Union Perceptions of the Impact of Change**

| | Strongly disagree | Disagree | Agree | Strongly agree | Correlation union/mgt. response |
|---|---|---|---|---|---|
| (1) The union involvement has reduced friction between the union and the company. | -- | 7/22% | 15/47% | 10/31% | .13 |
| | | (9/50%) | (6/33%) | (3/17%) | |
| (2) The union involvement has provided important information for making decisions. | -- | 8/24% | 21/64% | 4/12% | -.34 |
| | | (3/17%) | (12/67%) | (3/17%) | |
| (3) The union involvement has resulted in some major improvements in the productivity of the plant. | 1/3% | 14/44% | 15/47% | 2/6% | NA |
| | | (4/22%) | (8/44%) | (6/33%) | |
| (4) The union involvement has resulted in higher productivity in the plant. | 3/9% | 10/31% | 18/56% | 1/3% | .56** |
| | | (5/28%) | (7/39%) | (6/33%) | |
| (5) The union involvement has resulted in a better understanding of other labor-management issues. | -- | 3/10% | 19/61% | 9/29% | .20 |
| | | (4/22%) | (11/61%) | (3/17%) | |
| (6) The union has harassed the company without any benefit. | 8/25% | 21/66% | 2/6% | 1/3% | .34 |
| | (7/38%) | (9/50%) | (2/11%) | -- | |

(continued)

## Table 5-4 (continued)

|  | Strongly disagree | Disagree | Agree | Strongly agree | Correlation union/mgt. response |
|---|---|---|---|---|---|
| (7) The union has aided in bringing productivity issues to the attention of higher management officials. | -- | 11/33% | 19/58% | 3/9% | .48* |
|  | -- | (3/17%) | (8/44%) | (7/39%) |  |
| (8) The union involvement has aided in getting the workers to accept the suggested changes. | -- | 9/27% | 20/61% | 4/12% | -.01 |
|  | -- | (4/22%) | (11/61%) | (3/17%) |  |

|  | Very hostile | Somewhat hostile | Largely indifferent | Somewhat cooperative | Very cooperative | Corr. |
|---|---|---|---|---|---|---|
| (9) Overall, how would you rate the degree of hostility or cooperation that exists in the union-management relationship in your plant? | -- | 3/9% | 3/9% | 16/48% | 11/33% | .62** |
|  | (1/6%) | -- | (2/11%) | (11/61%) | (4/22%) |  |

|  | Not | Weakly | Generally | Strongly | Very strongly | Corr. |
|---|---|---|---|---|---|---|
| (10) In terms of your relationship with the union (mgt.) on the specific matters relating to *productivity*, how would you rate the degree of hostility or cooperation that occurs? | 1/3% | 3/9% | 5/15% | 18/55% | 6/18% | .54* |
|  | -- | (2/11%) | (2/11%) | (12/67%) | (2/11%) |  |
| (11) To what extent do you feel top management is committed to improving productivity in this plant? | -- | 3/10% | 6/19% | 8/26% | 14/45% | .38 |
|  | (1/6%) | (1/6%) | (8/44%) | (7/39%) | (1/6%) |  |

(12) Which of the following best describes the role you feel the union . . . should play in the area of plant productivity?

|  | Management | Union |
|---|---|---|
| The union should not be involved in any way in making major productivity decisions. | -- | -- |
| The union should be consulted before management makes major productivity decisions, but management makes the final decision. | 33/33% | 12/67% |
| The union should have about equal say in making major productivity decisions. | -- | 6/33% |

*p < .05, **p < .01

and 78 percent of the union respondents believed that their relationship on productivity issues was at least somewhat cooperative. Here again, there was significant agreement between respondents with the same organization ($r = .54$, $p < .05$).

One general area where there was less agreement was on the commitment of top management to improving plant productivity. Fifty-six percent of the union respondents did not believe management was strongly committed to productivity improvement. Only 6 percent believed that management was very strongly committed to productivity improvement, in contrast to 45 percent of the company respondents. Perhaps even more interesting, 29 percent of the management respondents did not believe that their superiors were strongly committed to productivity improvement.

There was universal agreement among managers on the role of the union on productivity issues with all 33 indicating that consultation was appropriate. Most union respondents agreed, however a substantial minority (33 percent) of the union respondents suggested that somewhat more involvement in productivity issues was appropriate.

On the individual perception items, union respondents tended to claim greater credit for improvements than management respondents were willing to recognize. This was particularly true on the specific issue of bringing productivity issues to the attention of higher management (Item 7) and on raising plant productivity (Item 9). These two issues, however, were the only two where there was general agreement between paired responses, $r = .48$ ($p < .05$) and $r = .56$ ($p < .01$), respectively. In addition, union respondents believed their organization deserved more credit for making major productivity improvements (Item 3).

Although both union and management respondents felt that unions did provide important information for making productivity decisions (Item 2), there was significant disagreement among the paired respondents, $r = -.34$, (n.s.). Also, on general issues related to labor-management relations, there was disagreement and low correlation between the management and union respondents. In Item 1, more union respondents (50 percent to 22 percent) did not believe the cooperative effort had reduced friction between the union and the company, and fewer (17 percent to 31 percent) did believe it had reduced friction. The correlation between the paired respondents was also low, $r = .13$, (n.s.). On "reaching a better understanding of other labor-management issues" (Item 5), a similar pattern of responses was evident, with management perceiving more benefit from the effort than the union.

This supports a proposition which has rarely been argued: that union-management cooperation works more to the advantage of management than the union and the workers (Peterson, Leitko & Miles 1981). Such a continued finding would have very significant policy implications for the practice of industrial relations. On the other hand, it may be that, as Kochan, Dyer, and Lipsky (1977) found in their study of safety committees, there is a tendency for management respondents to give a more socially acceptable response. If that were the case, it would certainly diminish the value of these findings. However, since both successful and unsuccessful programs were studied and there is reasonable variability in management responses, this probably did not occur in this research. In addition, on at least four key items there were significant correlations between the management and union responses.

## Conclusions

There is wide variation in the stimulus or reasons for union-management cooperation. But clearly, improving productivity, labor-management relations and wages are among the most important. In spite of this fact, cooperation will not occur if the stimulus issues can be resolved in collective bargaining. When the parties actually begin to move to a cooperative mode, neutrals or consultants facilitate the process.

One outcome of the upswing in cooperation has been an increase in employee participation at the workplace. Although employers are more willing to encourage this involvement, providing guarantees of employment security to workers appears to be as alien a concept as it has been historically. Consistent with this finding are two others on the potential and actual impact of cooperation. In both instances, management respondents perceived that cooperation was more instrumental in attaining program goals and believed there were more benefits from the cooperative effort than did the union respondents. In the next chapter, the impact of cooperation on organizational performance is discussed.

# NOTES

1. Two other local union presidents were interviewed, but these questionnaires were not usable.

# Chapter 6

# The Impact of
# Union-Management Cooperation

This chapter presents the results of the impact assessments of union-management cooperation programs. The chapter is divided into two parts. First is an overall summary of the performance of the entire sample of 38 plants. Although not all the sites provided data on all of the variables, the assembled data constitute one of the most in-depth evaluations available on this subject. In addition to the impact assessments, it was possible to consider some of the determinants of success. Readers are referred to the Schuster model, presented in chapter 2, that guided this research.

In Part Two, individual case histories are presented to illustrate the diversity of patterns in the practice of cooperative union-management relations. In this section, both successful and unsuccessful cases are included. Each case demonstrates why a plant effort was successful or some of the factors that contributed to its failure and demise. In addition to presenting statistical data of plant performances, visual data are utilized to further illustrate the impact of cooperative strategies.

## Summary of Performance Changes

*Impact Assessments*

This section summarizes the performance changes at all 38 research sites. Ten measures of performance were calculated.

129

These were time-series level and drift changes for productivity, quality, employment, turnover, absenteeism, tardiness, and grievances, plus data on the frequency of productivity bonus payments, program survival after two and five years, and rater effectiveness.

Two notes of caution must be made concerning the summarization of data. First, not all the sites provided data on all the variables. This was primarily the case on variables such as tardiness and grievances. Most firms do not keep records of this information, and many of those that could provide the information refused to do so because of the staff time needed to summarize it in a reasonable fashion. Second, as was discussed in chapter 4, some variables were not expected outcomes of the programs. Thus it would have been expected that productivity did not increase for some Labor-Management Committees since improving labor-management relations was the goal of the intervention and productivity improvement only a desired by-product.

Table 6-1 presents the summary of the level and drift changes. It should be recalled that a level change is an abrupt change in performance when the post-cooperation observations are compared with the pre-cooperation observations, while a drift change is a gradual change over time. Table 6-1 categorizes the performance variables into three categories: Positive Impact, No Impact, and Negative Impact.[1]

Of the 23 sites providing productivity data 11 (49 percent) had a positive level change, 10 (43 percent) had no change, and 2 (9 percent) were negative. On trend, 4 had positive changes, 12 had no change, and 7 a negative impact. Many in this latter group of 7 represent situations where there was a positive level change, followed by a decline. For the most part quality improved or was unchanged in both level and drift, although data were provided by only 4 sites.

A more interesting finding comes from the employment data. Historically, cooperation and productivity improve-

## Table 6-1
## Summary of Intervention Impact on Performance

| Performance measure | Level change | | | Trend change | | | Not available |
|---|---|---|---|---|---|---|---|
| | Positive impact | No impact | Negative impact | Positive impact | No impact | Negative impact | |
| Productivity | 11 (49%) | 10 (43%) | 2 (9%) | 4 (17%) | 12 (52%) | 7 (30%) | 15 |
| Quality | 1 (25%) | 2 (50%) | 1 (25%) | 2 (50%) | 2 (50%) | 0 (0%) | 34 |
| Employment | 6 (22%) | 17 (63%) | 4 (15%) | 7 (26%) | 14 (52%) | 6 (22%) | 11 |
| Turnover | -- | 6 (75%) | 2 (25%) | 1 (12.5%) | 5 (63%) | 2 (25%) | 30 |
| Absenteeism | 2 (29%) | 5 (71%) | -- | 2 (29%) | 4 (57%) | 1 (14%) | 31 |
| Tardiness | -- | -- | 1 | -- | 1 | -- | 37 |
| Grievances[a] | -- | 4 (100%) | -- | 1 (25%) | 2 (50%) | 1 (25%) | 29 |

a. Only includes the unionized sample.

ment have been feared by unions and workers as leading to a reduction in employment. Just the opposite was found in this case. In 23 of 27 firms, employment either increased or was unchanged following the intervention. Moreover, the long term effect was positive or unchanged in 21 situations. The analysis of this variable at each site was then compared with industry employment data. The result was that employment at the firm closely follows industry patterns and is probably most influenced by industry conditions. There were, however, several sites where the industry declined and the firm remained stable or increased. Interview data from management respondents suggest two reasons for this. First, that the cooperative effort, particularly gainsharing, had aided the plant in reducing unit costs, thus increasing its ability to compete and enabling it to acquire a larger market share. A second reason was a hesitancy to lay off workers because the benefits of cooperation might be lost. Union and worker militancy might increase as a result of the bitterness of a layoff.

The level of turnover declined in two instances and was unchanged in five. Tardiness declined in the one instance in which it was measured. Grievance rates were only improved in one of four sites studied, yet there were consistent reports of improved union-management relations. One interesting finding was that absenteeism was largely unchanged (71 percent) in level but did improve in two of seven instances.[2]

Table 6-2 summarizes the bonus payout frequency, survival (after two and five years), and rater effectiveness. Payment of a bonus is one measure of organizational productivity improvement. Of the 23 sites providing bonus data, 16 (70 percent) paid a bonus more than 50 percent of the time. Thirty-two (84 percent) cooperative programs survived the first two years, but four (11 percent) failed and two had not yet reached the two-year anniversary. Cooperation continued for five years in 14 of 16 sites where it had passed the two-year mark. Finally, rater effectiveness, defined as the extent to which the program was meeting its stated goals and objectives, was categorized by a single rater as being "very or somewhat successful," "not much effect," or "somewhat or very negative." Twenty-two (59 percent) cooperative experiments were characterized as having had a positive effect, 11 (29 percent) had not much effect, and 5 (13 percent) were rated as having had a negative effect.

Table 6-2
Bonus, Survival, and Rater Effectiveness Summary

|  | High | Low | NA |
|---|---|---|---|
| Bonus frequency | 16 (70%) | 7 (30%) | 6 |
|  | **Yes** | **No** | **NA** |
| Survival two years | 32 (84%) | 4 (37%) | 2 (5%) |
| five years | 14 (37%) | 2 (5%) | 22 (58%) |
|  | **Positive effect** | **No effect** | **Negative effect** |
| Rater effectiveness | 22 (59%) | 11 (29%) | 5 (13%) |

## Determinants of the Effectiveness of Cooperative Union-Management Programs

In chapter 2, five factors thought to influence cooperative union-management program success were slated for empirical investigation and were also utilized in the descriptive analysis later on in this chapter. These were guarantees of employment security; a structure for employee participation; the method, frequency, and amount of compensation provided by the program; an effective acceptance strategy; and an appropriate workplace technology. Some of these issues were also discussed in chapter 4 in the section on operational issues.

Because of the small sample size, it is not possible to conclusively report findings on the determinants of success. Although cross-tabulations were performed, and Chi-square statistics calculated, in many cases there were too many cells with too few observations to provide a meaningful analysis. However, the descriptive statistics do point to at least several variables that might be possible determinants of success. Each of these is briefly discussed as it relates only to productivity improvement, since sample size for most of the other variables is insufficient even for this level of analysis. Readers are cautioned that these results must be treated as preliminary.

*Employment security*

Guarantees of employment security were believed to influence program success because of historic worker fears that productivity improvement would reduce employment opportunities. The widespread reporting of Japanese management practices with their limited forms of lifetime employment have been suggested as a model for the American scene.

Contrary to the hypothesis, only three firms provided any type of employment security guarantees. One Scanlon Plan firm had a provision stating that no employees would lose their jobs with the company as a result of a Scanlon suggestion. Another firm provided supplemental unemployment benefits as part of a national agreement, but this was unrelated to the cooperative program. A third site had provisions for a "best efforts" clause which would have guaranteed very little job security. No additional firms provided any other guarantees of employment security. This is not to suggest that the subject was never discussed. It was a topic that both union and management respondents in sizable numbers raised. Many firms told their employees that increasing the economic performance of the company would have a positive effect upon their future employment prospects. Many union leaders entered into cooperative ventures with a strong hope and expectation that just such a result would occur.

Nevertheless, the evidence points to an absence of formal or informal provisions dealing with employment security issues.

### The structure for employee participation

It was hypothesized that opportunities for employee participation would influence cooperative program success. Moreover, the greater the degree of employee participation, the more successful the program would be. Because of small cell sizes, this variable was combined into two factors: departmental committees and plantwide/no opportunities for employee participation.

Twenty-seven organizations permitted some form of employee participation. However, the results for this proposition were largely inclusive. Of the 17 sites with some form of employee involvement in which productivity data were available, 8 had realized a position change in productivity level, seven had no change, and two were down.

Examining the relationship between participation and productivity may be too narrow in focus. Many of the firms with elaborate structures for worker involvement realized many nonproductivity improvements (such as quality and product design changes) through employee suggestions and projects. In many situations, simply providing employees the opportunity to be involved can produce a changed workplace environment. On the other hand, because Labor-Management Committees provide for limited forms of employee involvement, they were treated in the same manner as those sites with departmental committees. Unless L-MCs evolve to the stage of establishing departmental or sector subcommittees, they provide very little meaningful employee involvement. Thus, great care must be taken in interpreting these inconclusive findings.

It must be noted that of all the interventions studied, the Scanlon Plan seemed to have the strongest staying power. Whether this had to do with the bonus formula, the high level of employee participation, or some other factor is not known. What can be said, however, is that other productivity-sharing plans provided bonuses and had many other features similar to the Scanlon Plan. What appears to make the Scanlon Plan different is the commitment to, and institutionalization of, a high level of employee involvement.

*The method, frequency, and amount of compensation*

Since many cooperative union-management programs provided employees with an opportunity to share in productivity improvements, it was suggested that the manner in which employees were compensated would influence program success. It was hypothesized that large group (or plant-wide) sharing mechanisms, distributions of payouts, and, if available, large bonuses, would lead to program success.

Of the 38 firms (combined sample) studied, 28 contained some financial sharing provisions. There were 19 sites with plantwide distribution of productivity bonuses in which productivity data were available. Of these 19, 9 experienced an upward movement in productivity level, 8 were classified as unchanged, and 2 were down. Of the 4 sites with no sharing provisions, 2 experienced a productivity gain and 2 did not.

There were 18 sites with plantwide sharing provisions. Productivity data was available for 11. Of these 11, productivity increased in 7, was unchanged in 3, and was lower in 1. There were 9 sites with group distribution of bonuses. Of the 7 where productivity data were available, productivity was higher at 1 site, unchanged at 5 sites and lower at 1.

Thus, it would appear, subject to sample limitations, that cooperative programs with plantwide sharing provisions are preferable to those with group sharing provisions. The rationale for a plantwide distribution strategy is to encourage teamwork, cooperation, and ease of bonus administration. Plantwide sharing of bonus earnings eliminates a major problem that was detected at those plants with group-based distributions. The group-based plans generally provide differential bonus earnings and this can create a problem of internal equity and a high level of dissension regarding the program. This is particularly true when there is skepticism as to the accuracy of the bonus sharing formula or standards of performance.

*An effective acceptance strategy*

An effective acceptance strategy was defined as one that included an active training program for first-level supervision and union stewards, use of external consultants, and an effective mechanism to communicate the activities of the cooperative program.

Twenty sites (61 percent) had training programs for supervisors and stewards to facilitate the implementation of the cooperative program. This is very important since such training programs tend to produce a better understanding of the goals and implications of the cooperative programs. Training programs at this level of the organization can also work to dismantle some of the hostility that often exists between supervisors and stewards.

Productivity data were available at 12 of the 20 sites with training efforts. Of these 12, productivity increased at 8 sites and was unchanged in 4. Of those 13 sites where no training was utilized, productivity data were available for 10. Of those, productivity increased at 2, was unchanged at 6, and was lower at 2. Thus, it would appear that training programs should be conducted as part of any cooperative labor-management intervention.

Neutrals or consultants were involved in 28 of the 33 interventions (85 percent). Productivity data were available for 20 sites. Of these, 10 experienced a productivity gain, 8 were unchanged, and 2 were lower. Third parties play an important role because companies and unions often do not fully understand how to organize the cooperative processes. Expert consultants are almost always essential in designing productivity-sharing formulas. Not only do they provide financial expertise, but they also enhance the fairness and equity of the bonus.

There was a great deal of variability in how each of the sites communicated the activities of their program and it was decided not to attempt to categorize them. It is possible, however, to note some of the more effective approaches. The successful productivity-sharing plans took the employees away from their work stations on company time to explain the mechanics of their plans. These sites also printed booklets describing their plans in detail and including many commonly asked questions and answers. Many firms with productivity-sharing plans stop work to publicly announce the bonus each month and thereafter spend considerable time explaining to their employees in plant and departmental meetings why a bonus was earned or why the company and employees failed to perform at a level to earn a bonus.

Most firms, regardless of type of cooperative program, utilize bulletin boards and circulation of minutes of meetings to keep participants informed of activities in other areas. Elected members of employee committees are often permitted to bring visitors (other workers) to committee meetings to increase their understanding of the cooperative process. One large innovative firm has made the agendas of its labor-management subcommittees part of its management information system. Thus, the plant manager receives a periodic update of activities. When a project has failed to receive a management response after 30 or 60 days, the plant manager begins to ask questions.

*Technology*

Technology was hypothesized to influence the success of cooperative union-management programs for two reasons. First, although these interventions change the structure of the organization, it was believed that the structure and technology should be congruent. Second, and most important, it was believed that in more capital intensive or mechanized operations, workers would have fewer opportunities to provide inputs into the production processes. This would reduce the effectiveness of the cooperative effort, particularly where a significant degree of employee participation was expected.

The technology variable was measured using a Woodward scale and later recast into more mechanized (mass production industries—production runs of over one week) and less mechanized (more customized operations and those with production runs of less than one week).

Productivity data were available for 10 sites that were less mechanized and 12 that were more mechanized. The results were contrary to what was expected. Of the less mechanized sites, 3 had productivity gains and 7 were unchanged. Of the more mechanized sites, 7 had productivity gains, 3 were unchanged, and 2 were lower. One interpretation of this finding may be that cooperative interventions can be effective in a variety of situations; however, when workers increase their efforts, the impact on productivity is greater in more automated assembly situations.

*Other factors related to success*

Type of ownership appeared to influence success, with the subsidiaries of large corporations more likely to achieve increases in productivity than family owned or corporate enterprises. Perhaps these firms have more resources and more capable management to facilitate the implementation of the interventions. In addition, productivity level changes were more likely to occur with older work forces, but trend changes were more likely to result with younger work populations.

## Case Studies of Cooperation

Ten case studies are presented in this section.[3] Each case study was chosen because it offers some lesson or set of conditions to foster cooperation. Several cases were selected because they highlight the difficulties and pitfalls that caused the interventions to fail.

Case study 1 is the classic case of cooperation to save the plant and the jobs of the workforce. Case study 2 demonstrates that a cooperative strategy can be used to motivate the workforce and improve the quality of worklife. Case study 3 provides evidence that it may take time for the full benefits of cooperation to be realized. Case study 4 demonstrates the successful implementation of a labor-management committee. Case study 5 combines three union-management relationships that have been in existence for more than ten years.

Cases 6-10 highlight the difficulties and problems of cooperation. Case study 6 shows how a successful effort can lose its effectiveness when fairness and equity in the bonus formula are lost. Case study 7 demonstrates that not all interventions may be appropriate to all organizational settings and union-management relationships. Case study 8 outlines the failure of a labor-management committee to adequately address the organization's problems, while 9 shows how traditional labor-management issues can interfere with the implementation and acceptance of QWL concepts. Finally, case study 10 is a warning of the potential misuse of gain-sharing.

Each case study contains a brief description of the plant and its cooperative effort. For each case there is a statistical summary table which includes point estimates of the level and drift of time-series at time $t = 0$ with associated t-statistics. Estimation of post-intervention change in level and drift with associated t-statistic permits an assessment of the impact of the cooperative union-management efforts. The numbers identifying each firm correspond to the site numbers in table 3-2 and 3-3, thus enabling readers to further examine the characteristics of each plant.

## Case Study 1: Cooperation to Save the Plant

Site 8 was a manufacturer of abrasive cut-off wheels for cutting steel and other metals. The plant employed 140 production workers. In the late 1960s, the plant began to suffer financial difficulties. During the period 1968-71 there were four wildcat strikes and several work slowdowns. The plant had operated with negotiated production standards which were the source of considerable tension between management and the union. In 1971, after contract negotiations failed, the corporation announced plans to close the plant for economic reasons.

As a result of the decision to close the plant, the state government and the international union district director became involved. Through a series of hastily arranged tripartite negotiations, conditions were reached under which the plant could remain open. Prior to the decision to close, the Scanlon Plan had been under consideration but was rejected by the corporation. Plant management was able to convince corporate officials of the viability of the Plan as an alternative to closing. The union also offered its full cooperation to improve productivity and an end to negotiated work standards. In return, management agreed to contractual language which would preclude the layoff of workers as a result of suggestions from the Scanlon committees.

The philosophy of the Scanlon Plan was expressed in the program handbook:

> The SPIP recognizes each employee as an individual—each able to contribute to the group

something more than just day-to-day work. The plan provides a way to communicate ideas and suggestions to management, and to share in the benefits of the improvements. Under the SPIP, the opportunity is provided for people to say how their own jobs might best be done. It means all employees thinking a little bit more about who gets the job after his or her operation and how the job might be made easier for them. The plan means that the older, more experienced employee gives his ideas on how the job should be done to the new employee. It means that the younger employee may be more physically able to help or make his contribution to the older employee. It means that management makes decisions on what is good for the company and not on what is good for any individual.

Site 8's experience was analyzed for the period January 1969-December 1973, with the intervention point being March 1971, the start of the Scanlon Plan. As table 6-3 indicates, there was an abrupt rise in productivity to a higher and statistically significant level ($t = 8.14$, $p < .001$) following introduction of the Scanlon Plan. This change is shown even more dramatically in figure 6-1. Readers may notice that the sharp increase in productivity began in the month prior to the formal installation of the plan. This can be explained by the threat posed by the shutdown and the decision of the company to pay a bonus for the prior month's productivity performance. For the first three years of the Plan, bonuses averaged 4.0 percent, 4.4 percent, and 9.3 percent. The firm was unable to provide monthly employment data. Instead, annual data were provided. There was a layoff of 20 percent of the bargaining units' employees in the six months prior to the institution of the Plan. Following the introduction of the Scanlon Plan employment stabilized.

**Figure 6-1**
**Site 8 Productivity**

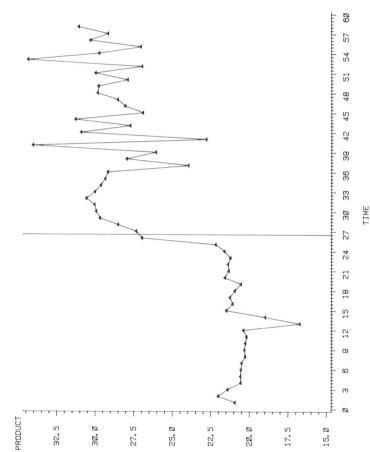

Table 6-3
Site 8 Summary
(Case 1)

|  | Level | T-Stat | Lev Chg | T-Stat |
|---|---|---|---|---|
| Productivity<br>(N = 58, df = 54) | 19.94 | 30.97 | 6.89 | 8.14+ |
|  | **Drift** | **T-Stat** | **Dft Chg** | **T-Stat** |
|  | 0.07 | 1.70 | -0.05 | -0.97 |

+ p < .001

This is a classic case of union-management cooperation to save the business and in turn save the jobs of union members. Scanlon enthusiasts have claimed that productivity can "go through the roof." Although that is unlikely to be a universal result, this firm certainly experienced a marked increase in productivity, along with no reduction in employment following the Plan's introduction. In subsequent years, the Scanlon Plan continued to be successful and ten years following its installation remained active.

## Case Study 2: Cooperation to Motivate the Workforce and Improve the Quality of Worklife

Site 4 is a plant of a large multinational corporation. The plant housed two separate operating divisions. The larger division manufactured original equipment for jet aircraft engines, while the smaller division rehabilitated service-run turbine parts to provide additional flying hours for the aircraft. From an organizational perspective, the two divisions were distinct units. Each had a separate division manager with key operating personnel reporting to one of these managers, and both were independent profit centers. However, the divisions shared common staff departments, for example, accounting and personnel. More important, there was only one union representing all the employees at the site and they were covered by a common collective bargaining agreement. There was one Scanlon Plan encompassing all employees of both divisions.

In two other situations in this study in which the management structure was similar, both companies opted to utilize separate plans. Thus one company had two Rucker Plans in nearby plants, while another company utilized four Improshare Plans with four operating divisions on the same site. In both instances, the employees constituted one bargaining unit with a single collective agreement and separation into distinct plans caused friction, particularly when differential bonuses were earned. The single-plan strategy utilized at this site would seem to be the preferred one.

The plant had 900-1000 nonsupervisory production employees who had organized an independent union in 1952. The history of labor relations at the plant had been relatively peaceful. Strikes had been rare and of a short duration. Although the union was an independent one, it had negotiated continuous improvements in its contracts. Wages and benefits were among the highest in the community.

The stimulus for the Plan stemmed from corporate encouragement for workplace innovation and the desire of local management to motivate a somewhat older workforce and to improve productivity. The plant's top management was strongly committed to the Scanlon philosophy. The union leadership also saw benefits (greater role in the operation of the plant, increased wages) for its members. This led to the development, implementation and continued strengthening of the structure for employee participation. This site permits a detailed examination of the Scanlon Plan in operation.

All Scanlon Plans have a two-level committee structure—Production Committees designed along departmental lines and a higher level Screening Committee. There were 26 Production Committees: 14 first shift, 10 second shift, and 2 third shift committees. There were also committees of salaried and clerical workers. The Production Committees ranged in size from two to five employees elected (one-year term) to serve on each committee and one managerial employee appointed as chairperson by the company. The committees met at least once a month on company time. To increase employee participation, each elected member was permitted to invite an employee from his/her area to attend Production Committee meetings. The Production Committees were responsible for discussing problems and responding to suggestions within their jurisdictions. There were five possible dispositions for employee suggestions:

(1) *Accept and implement a suggestion.* This can be done when the cost does not exceed $225. When a suggestion is accepted, it is the responsibility of the committee to inform the suggestor.

(2) *Reject the suggestion.* The Production Committee is responsible for informing the suggestor of the reasons for the rejection.

(3) *Accept the suggestion and put it under investigation.* This is done when there is not enough information to determine whether the savings involved would offset the costs of putting it into effect.

(4) *Accept the suggestion and refer it to the Screening Committee.* This occurs when the implementation costs exceed $225.

(5) *Reject the suggestion and refer it to the Screening Committee.* These are situations in which there is a difference of opinion between the chairperson of a Production Committee and an employee member over the merits of a suggestion. It should be noted that the chairpersons of the Production Committees are appointed by management and maintain veto power over decisions reached.

In most Scanlon Plans, when a suggestion falls within the jurisdiction of another Production Committee, it is normally referred to the Screening Committee for a decision. At this plant the approach differed. Where there was a potential jurisdictional conflict concerning a suggestion, it was the responsibility of the chairperson to obtain approval from other Production Committees. Only when there was an actual conflict was the suggestion referred to the Screening Committee. Thus an attempt was made to maintain decision-making at the lowest level of the organization.

Selection of employee members for the Screening Committee was also a function of the Production Committees. The Production Committees selected an hourly representative to attend an organizational meeting of the Screening Committee. The first and second shifts had 14 and 10 Production Committees, respectively. At the Screening Committee organizational meeting the 11 representatives from the first shift must select five persons from their group to serve on the Screening Committee. The second shift had four seats. The third shift and office each had one seat. Those Production Committees with no active members on the Screening Committee are permitted to send a guest each month.

The Screening Committee (organizational chart below) had 21 members. The 21 included 11 elected employee members, 9 managerial employees, and the union president and a union representative appointed by him. The Screening Committee meets at least once a month also on company time. Its responsibilities include assisting the Production Committees, reviewing the monthly bonus calculations with a view toward identifying problems and opportunities, and considering potential business problems. As with the Production Committees, management maintains decisionmaking authority on the Screening Committee.

---

### Two General Managers to Serve as Committee Chairpersons

| | |
|---|---|
| Manufacturing Manager | Union President |
| Industrial Engineering Manager | Union Board Member |
| Engineering Manager | 1st Shift Production Committee |
| Production Control Manager | Representatives (5) |
| Quality Control Manager | 2nd Shift Production Committee |
| Personnel | Representatives (4) |
| Maintenance Superintendent | 3rd Shift Production Committee |
| | Representatives (1) |
| | Office Departments |
| | Representatives (1) |

---

Through the first 45 months of meetings, employees had made 1884 suggestions. Seventy percent had been accepted and 7 percent were under review. In the first three years of the Plan, bonuses averaged 5.9 percent, 6.5 percent, and 7.1 percent, respectively.

Productivity and employment data for Site 4 were analyzed for the periods January 1973-December 1977, and December 1972-December 1977, respectively, with the intervention occurring in May 1975. This analysis is summarized in table 6-4. Productivity was measured separately for each division. For the manufacturing division there was a significant upward shift in the level of the time-series following introduction of the Plan ($t = 2.09$, $p < .05$). Over time there was a positive, although not statistically significant, upward trend in the series ($t = .60$). The productivity analysis for the repair division revealed that the productivity increase was more gradual, as indicated by the change in drift ($t = 3.38$, $p < .001$). Employment remained stable, with almost no change in the level ($t = .31$, n.s.) or the drift ($t = -.06$, n.s.).

This Scanlon Plan demonstrates that internal, noneconomic factors can be a sufficiently powerful stimulus to induce effective union-management cooperation. A critical factor in the success of this Scanlon Plan is the com-

**Table 6-4**
**Site 4 Summary**
**(Case 2)**

| | Level | T-Stat | Lev Chg | T-Stat | Drift | T-Stat | Dft Chg | T-Stat |
|---|---|---|---|---|---|---|---|---|
| Productivity manufacturing (N = 65, df = 61) | .92 | 4.81 | .40 | 2.09* | 0.03 | .81 | 0.02 | 0.66 |
| Productivity repair (N = 65, df = 61) | 3.59 | 15.88 | 0.49 | 1.56 | -0.06 | -5.15 | 0.06 | 3.38 + |
| Employment (N = 61, df = 57) | 105.81 | 26.84 | 1.21 | 0.31 | -0.08 | -0.06 | -0.09 | -0.05 |

*p < .05, + p < .001

mitment of top management toward employee involvement in the daily and long range operation of the company. This commitment has manifested itself in the creation of an environment and structure to produce the desired outcome. Also important has been the maintenance of a sense of equity by virtue of the payment of bonuses stemming from productivity increases.

## Case Study 3: Evidence of a Delayed Effect

Site 16 (100 bargaining unit employees) designs and manufactures automated, continuous roll-to-roll processing machinery systems for converting the physical composition of paper, boards, film, foil, plastics and textiles into finished products. In recent years, labor relations had not been good. In 1973, there was a 12-day strike, and in the subsequent round of negotiations (1976) a 17-week strike occurred. Both company and union representatives agreed that problems and inequities in the plant's individual incentive system were the cause. During the strike, employees, mostly skilled machinists, took jobs elsewhere. After the strike, turnover continued at a high rate when a large company opened nearby offering similar employment at much higher rates of pay.

As the 1979 negotiations neared, both sides prepared for another strike. In addition, the company argued that under the existing incentive program, workers were earning too high a premium for "below standard" performance, while the union reported that the existing payment system (base plus incentive) did not permit employees to realize sufficient earnings.

During the 1979 negotiations, the company proposed the introduction of the Rucker Plan. The union, which had vast experience at the national level with productivity-sharing plans, agreed to the Plan subject to the establishment of a new hourly pay rate. An agreement was reached to establish a six-month average of individual earnings under the old incentive system, plus an 8 percent pay increase.

The Rucker Plan did not deviate from the traditional Rucker form as discussed elsewhere. There was a suggestion program, a committee system, and the productivity-sharing bonus formula. Employee suggestions are the responsibility of the Idea Coordinator, the manager of industrial engineering, who assigns the suggestion to an appropriate manager or professional employee for study, analysis, and a recommendation.

There was a single employee committee, the Group Incentive Committee (GIC), with 10 employees chosen by management serving four-month rotating terms. Initially three criteria were used for selection: geographic dispersion, status among the hourly workforce, and in some cases initial opposition to the Plan. The union president is a permanent committee member. The GIC meets twice a month on company time. At the first meeting each month, the committee discusses ideas that have been submitted and at least one major subject, for example, a scrap or turnover. The second monthly meeting reviews actions taken as a result of the first meeting and discusses the most recent bonus.

The productivity bonus formula was based upon a five-year analysis of the plant's financial performance. The Rucker formula is based upon the relationship between bargaining unit payroll and production value. The following calculations are made to achieve a base:

Production Value = Sales Value of Output - Materials and Supplies

$$\text{Rucker Base} = \frac{\text{Pay and Benefits of Bargaining Unit Personnel}}{\text{Production Value}}$$

The relationship was 22.09 percent. The productivity bonus is then measured by

Production Value x Base - Actual Pay and Benefits.

One third of an earned bonus is set aside for deficit accounting periods. Because the plant produces large equipment in stages, the bonus is calculated and paid on a quarterly basis, in a separate check. The only nonbargaining unit employees in the Plan are supervisors, but they are paid from company, rather than bargaining unit, earnings. Under the Rucker formula, improvements in quality increase production value which is shared with the employees. The results showed that there was a modest increase in productivity.[4] More interesting was the impact on employee absenteeism and quality, which are reported in table 6-5.

Employment was analyzed for the period January 1977 - May 1982. There was a sharp increase in employment following introduction of the Plan ($t = 3.40$, $p < .001$), with a slight downturn thereafter ($t = .97$, n.s.). The industry also experienced a corresponding but smaller increase in employment ($t = 1.23$, n.s.), but then a substantial deterioration in trend over time ($t = -2.83$, $p < .01$). Thus the plan had greater employment stability than did the industry.

Absenteeism (unexcused absences ÷ workforce size) was analyzed for the period January 1977 - May 1982. There was no change in the level of absenteeism and only a modest improvement in the trend. Quality (the percentage of rework hours to direct labor hours) was analyzed for the period April 1978 - May 1982. Once again, there was no change in the level of quality following the intervention, and a limited improvement in the trend. In both instances, interesting and potentially important findings occurred from the three-month delayed analysis. Absenteeism declined significantly ($t = 2.07$, $p < .05$) and continued a negative trend ($t = -.85$, n.s.). The improvement in quality was also very significant with a substantial improvement in the trend ($t = -2.37$, $p < .01$). These results are shown visually in figures 2 and 3.

Cook and Campbell (1979) have suggested that the impact of an intervention into a complex organizational situation might not be immediately felt. When considering change in unionized settings there may be a delayed effect on employee work attitudes, behavior, and performance during an in-

## Table 6-5
## Site 16 Summary
## (Case 3)

| | Level | T-Stat | Lev Chg | T-Stat | Drift | T-Stat | Dft Chg | T-Stat |
|---|---|---|---|---|---|---|---|---|
| Employment (N=65, df=61) | 105.38 | 25.34 | 14.15 | 3.40+ | -0.14 | -0.16 | -1.23 | -0.97 |
| Employment control (N=64, df=60) | 118.97 | 95.02 | 1.55 | 1.23 | 0.41 | 1.39 | -1.06 | -2.83** |
| Absenteeism (N=64, df=60) | 3.47 | 9.11 | -0.09 | -0.22 | -0.00 | -0.19 | -0.04 | -1.54 |
| Absenteeism delayed effect | 3.48 | 10.39 | -0.78 | -2.07* | -0.00 | -0.16 | -0.02 | -0.85 |
| Quality (N=50, df=46) | 9.20 | 6.20 | 0.42 | 0.29 | 0.04 | 0.20 | -0.28 | -1.13 |
| Quality delayed effect | 10.18 | 8.24 | 1.79 | 1.38 | -0.03 | -0.32 | -0.30 | -2.37** |

*p<.05, **p<.01, +p<.001

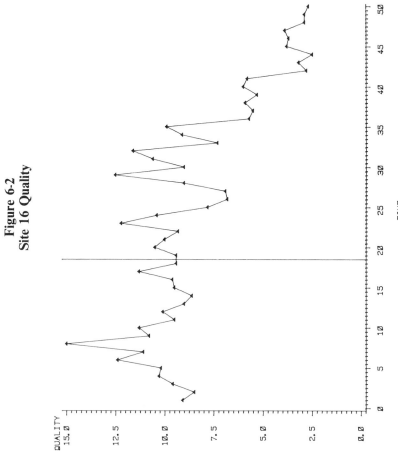

**Figure 6-2**
**Site 16 Quality**

**Figure 6-3**
**Site 16 Absenteeism**

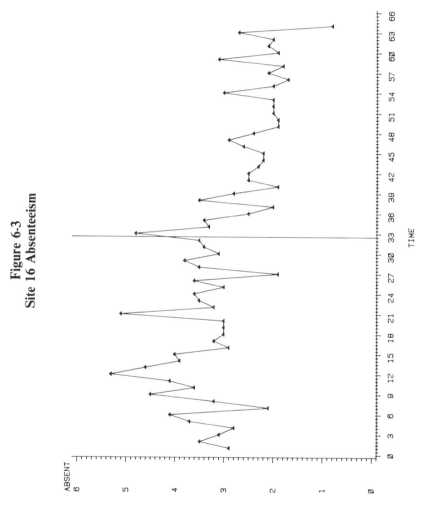

terim period in which employees become fully aware and educated, and a delay required for a high level of acceptance, trust and expertise to develop. This demonstrates that it may take time for productivity and Quality of Worklife programs to mature and realize their full capacity for improved employee performance.

Although it was not possible to directly measure the quality of the labor-management relationship, the last two rounds of contract negotiations (1979 and 1982) were concluded peacefully. Because the two previous experiences (1973 and 1976) resulted in strikes over issues which the Plan was designed to address, it may be concluded that the Plan at least partially contributed to improved labor-management relations.

Since the inception of the Plan, there have been over 400 suggestions processed with 70 percent having been accepted. Quarterly bonuses have been paid less than 50 percent of the time but have been very large (in excess of 20 percent three times).

The success of this intervention was influenced by several factors. First, there was a strong stimulus for change. The two preceding rounds of contract negotiations had resulted in labor disputes, one of which lasted 17 weeks. There was also a concern about high labor turnover and low wages. Second, both the company and the union were committed to a jointly approved solution to the problem. Third, the parties utilized competent consultants for the development and implementation of the Plan. The consultants helped to maintain equity in the bonus formula. Fourth, the level of employee participation, although not as great as with other interventions, for example, Scanlon Plans and Quality Circles, appeared to be congruent with the preferences of both the employees and the management. Finally, the union was directly involved in the supervision of the Plan through membership on the Group Incentive Committee.

## Case Study 4: The Successful Use
## of a Labor-Management Committee

Site 23 is a tire manufacturer with 800 bargaining unit employees. During 1976, the industry suffered from over-capacity, and in 1977, the plant was threatened with a loss of jobs due to industry competition.

In 1977 the Union's Bargaining Committee and the top plant management met to discuss ways and means to improve productivity. As a result of these discussions, the union agreed to renegotiate work rules through the formal collective bargaining process. After the 1977 negotiations were concluded, the union and the company continued to maintain monthly meetings to discuss problems and to avoid personality conflicts. These meetings continued until mid-1978 when top management stopped attending the meetings and instead, was represented by middle managers. Thereafter, regular meetings were discontinued.

In March 1980, economic conditions forced the layoff of 250 employees. Meetings were begun to discuss ongoing difficulties. Plant management projected a loss of more than $11 million. The company told the union that approximately $5 million of the projected loss was due to labor costs, productivity, and operating difficulties, while over $6 million was due to difficulties in sales, marketing and distribution.

In November 1980, the Union agreed to $1.05 an hour wage reduction, by virtue of an immediate curtailment in the cost-of-living adjustment of $.55 and a $.50 deferment in future cost-of-living payments. To offset this decrease, the company and union agreed to a gainsharing program which would compensate the employees for their loss. In addition, the parties requested that the community's Area Labor-Management Committee (A L-MC) begin working with them to fully develop the Labor-Management Committee (L-MC) concept. This case offers the opportunity to view the L-MC process in action.

The Labor-Management Committee is an extension of the collective bargaining process and is composed of top management members, including the plant manager and members of his operating staff and the local union president and other key elected officials of the local. The top management official and the local union president act as the L-MC co-chairpersons. There are also departmental and ad hoc subcommittees. The L-MC is designed to bring these actors together to improve the working relationship between the company and the union by fostering attitudinal change. Once this has been achieved, other significant issues can be addressed and the L-MC becomes a vehicle for organizational change.

The role of the A L-MC is to provide technical assistance to aid the parties in implementing and making effective the in-plant L-MC. The A L-MC provided, at no cost to the company or union, an expert third-party consultant. This individual helped guide the parties through the initial stages of gaining commitment and acceptance of the concept and, thereafter, helped them to develop a process for addressing substantive problems. The eventual goal of the A L-MC is to educate the principals so that they are able to function independently, that is without the assistance of the third party.

At the outset, the L-MC process is designed to get each side to understand the opponents role and the difficulties each faces. The goal is to reach a stage where the adversary process is de-emphasized and the parties are able to jointly address problems facing the company, the union, and the workforce. It is expected that the parties will acknowledge this change, as was the case at Site 23.

The initial process forces the parties to work together. The L-MC begins modestly by developing the local mechanics of the process (meeting times, places, participants, etc.); getting the individual actors to agree to meet; setting a flexible agenda; and informing everyone, management and union, of the activities taking place. Most L-MCs initially focus on minor irritants such as physical improvements to work and non-work areas. Because there had been a short-lived L-MC effort three years before at Site 23, many of these issues were easier to resolve. The important point, however, is that the L-MC process teaches both sides to behave in a more sophisticated manner. Although either side can always revert to its existing rights under the collective bargaining agreement (e.g., the company could assert its right to manage the business), the process requires that the parties be more attentive to their counterpart's problems, concerns, and point of view.

At Site 23, the parties moved more quickly into substantive issues of productivity, attendance, quality, management control systems, scheduling, and implementing departmental committees.

There are six departmental subcommittees consisting of two to four employees and two to four managers. Stewards and rank-and-file members represent the union on these committees. Ad hoc committees are created to examine specific problems.

The L-MC and departmental subcommittees have the effect of collapsing the organizational structure. The union leadership and its members have direct and frequent contact with top management decisionmakers. Information and problems are allowed to surface and potential solutions cannot be ignored. At this site, an effort is made to force the subcommittees to make decisions rather than sending them to the main committee. The main L-MC also consults the subcommittees on issues with plantwide implications. Thus communication and involvement are increased.

An example of the change and innovation at Site 23 is the manner in which employee attendance was addressed. To complement the existing negotiated disciplinary procedure for absenteeism, the parties established an Attendance

Review Council. The Council consisted of three rank-and-file volunteers and three supervisors who counseled employees with irregular attendance. Where needed, corrective services were provided. The Council could not discipline employees but did replace a contractually negotiated absence point system for employee discipline. The Council in no way abrogates management's right to discipline or discharge employees under the collective bargaining agreement.

At this site, the L-MCs departmental subcommittees and ad hoc committees closely resemble the structure of the Scanlon Committees and Quality Circles. There is, however, a very significant and important distinction. With Scanlon Plans, Quality Circles, and Rucker Plans, the union primarily has an oversight responsibility. The local union president serves on the Screening Committees with perhaps another union official, but for the most part, this is the extent of direct union involvement. In most Scanlon and Rucker Plans and Quality Circles, there is a conscious effort to keep union stewards off the committees. The rationale is to separate the cooperative process from the traditional adversary processes of the grievance procedure and negotiations machinery. In this regard, L-MCs are very different; the union is an equal partner in the operation of the entire process. An effort is made to immerse stewards along with rank-and-file workers into the process. Organizational change comes as a direct result of this involvement and the union, as the co-partner in the L-MC, is both responsible for failures, as well as entitled to claim credit for success. In short, both sides have ownership of the effort. This should be contrasted with many of the other interventions studied which were in large part management directed with union oversight responsibility.

The L-MC process at Site 23 helped the parties overcome several difficult issues which might have caused the demise of other cooperative efforts. An example was the gainsharing program. The bonus formula was based on equivalent pounds per man hour augmented by savings on waste. This formula was the most accurate measure of productivity of all the sites investigated in this research. However, the formula required the plant, which had been performing at about 80 percent of standard, to be above 100 percent of standard for a two-month period, and three six-month periods, thereafter. Employees would receive 50 percent of the cost reductions that resulted from increased productivity above the 100 percent.

Thus there was to be a biannual bonus with no reward for incremental improvement and poor weeks and months during this period offsetting good performance in other months. No bonus was earned for any period during the first 12 months. Productivity during this period initially improved, but performance never reached the point at which a bonus could be achieved.

This caused disenchantment and led much of the workforce to abandon hopes of earning a bonus. After a period of four to six months, productivity, which had increased to approximately 90 percent, declined to previous levels. The cause of this problem was the construction of the formula. Rather than rewarding and reinforcing incremental improvement, only the excess above the 100 percent goal would entitle the employees to receive a bonus. The period of time for measurement of performance, six months, was unusually long. This combination had the effect of creating a disincentive when no bonus was earned. At several other sites studied, this might have caused cooperation to be terminated. However, because the relationship between the company and the union had improved—in particular, the personal relationship between the key actors had been strengthened—the parties were able to discuss their problem and arrive at a mutually successful solution. That solution was to reward incremental improvement using a four-week moving average payout system. In the second year of the gainsharing, bonuses ranged from $.09-$.46 per hour, with an average of $.30 per hour.

Table 6-6 sumarizes the plant's performance. Productivity measured as equivalent pounds per hour, was analyzed for the period January 1979 - July 1982. Productivity increased slightly following the intervention (t = .93, n.s.), but increased significantly over time (t = 4.12, p < .001).

Employment and turnover were measured for the period January 1978 - June 1981. Employment, after remaining unchanged following the program's introduction (t = -.48, n.s.), showed a positive gain over time (t = 1.43, n.s.). At the same time, industry employment remained unchanged (t = .23 and .44, both n.s.). Both plant turnover (t = .37 and -.29, both n.s.) and industry turnover (t = -.96 and .19, both n.s.) remained unchanged.

Quality for both the major and minor products at the plant was measured by a ratio of scrap dollar value to output dollar value. The major product's quality was analyzed for the period January 1978 - December 1981. Scrap for the major product was unchanged following the program's start-up (t = -.78, n.s.). Over time, though, the decrease in scrap approached statistical significance (t = -1.53, n.s.). The amount of scrap for the minor product decreased to a similar degree initially (t = -1.52, n.s.), while the trend remained unchanged over time (t = .11, n.s.).

Absenteeism was measured for the period January 1978 - June 1982. Absenteeism remained unchanged throughout the time-series analysis (t = .82 and -.50, both n.s.).

This site is a very good example of a L-MC being used to change the organization. First, attitudinal change took place, along with the development of a structure for change. Thereafter, the parties began to address obstacles to organizational effectiveness. In contrast to most other

Table 6-6
Site 23 Summary
(Case 4)

| | Level | T-Stat | Lev Chg | T-Stat | Drift | T-Stat | Dft Chg | T-Stat |
|---|---|---|---|---|---|---|---|---|
| Productivity (N = 43, df = 39) | 58.56 | 44.93 | 1.37 | 0.93 | -0.19 | -1.96 | 0.55 | 4.12 + |
| Employment | 158.82 | 56.81 | -1.42 | -0.48 | -0.99 | -1.73 | 1.93 | 1.43 |
| Employment control (N = 42, df = 38) | 128.92 | 63.75 | 0.23 | 0.10 | -0.55 | -1.38 | 0.37 | 0.44 |
| Turnover | 0.72 | 7.72 | 0.08 | 0.37 | -0.00 | -0.76 | -0.01 | -0.29 |
| Turnover control (N = 42, df = 38) | 0.40 | 2.00 | -0.20 | -0.96 | -0.00 | -0.00 | 0.01 | 0.19 |
| Quality-major (N = 48, df = 44) | 2.03 | 5.54 | -0.03 | -0.78 | 0.04 | 0.99 | -0.11 | -1.53 |
| Quality-minor (N = 43, df = 39) | 2.67 | 1.26 | -7.38 | -1.52 | 0.31 | 2.97 | 0.09 | 0.11 |
| Absenteeism (N = 56, df = 52) | 0.08 | 7.11 | 0.01 | 0.82 | -0.00 | -0.01 | -0.00 | -0.50 |

+ p < .001

change efforts studied, the union shares ownership of the process with the company.

There has been an improvement in organizational performance, but this gives rise to the "black box" issue. Was it the gainsharing or the L-MC that produced the improvements? The answer is probably both. Certainly the gainsharing rewarded improved performance, but the L-MC process facilitated and created an environment in which organizational efficiency could be fostered. Moreover, many of the improvements in productivity were the result of the work done by the departmental and ad hoc subcommittees. Finally, the Area Labor-Management Committee provided much of the expertise to help the parties make the L-MC process work.

## Case Study 5: Three Cases of Long Term Success

This segment combines the experiences of three companies with long term cooperative efforts. All three have Scanlon Plans. The Plans are 15, 12 and 29 years in length, respectively. All three Plans operate in the traditional Scanlon format.

Site 28 employs 370 hourly workers and produces automated assembly systems, special balancing machines, and vertical automatic production lathes. The Scanlon Plan was an outgrowth of a 13-week strike over union demands for a wage increase and a group incentive system.

Both the company and the union were familiar with the Scanlon Plan. The plant was at one time owned by a local manufacturer who had a "successful" Scanlon Plan in another location. No serious consideration was given to alternative systems. The Scanlon Plan was seen as a mechanism for tying increased earnings to productivity. Since the union proposed the concept, gaining employee acceptance was not difficult.

The Plan began in January 1968 and has eight Production Committees and one Screening Committee. Even though the Plan has matured, it continues to process 100-150 suggestions per year with an annual acceptance rate from 50-70 percent. Ideas that do not exceed $300 can be implemented by the Production Committees. Suggestions that will cost more than $300 require Screening Committee approval. Aside from this situation, the plant manager actively discourages any suggestions going beyond the Production Committee level.

The committee system has developed into the most effective line of communication between management and the employees. Through the committees, management makes a determined effort to keep the employees aware of the financial position, including profitability, of the company. Management officials felt that the committee system has made the employees ". . . much more aware of what it takes to run the company," and that the employees see a relationship between productivity and profitability, this helping to create an atmosphere of trust and understanding. Both management officials and the union chairperson agreed that the opportunity for employee participation had played a key role in what they felt had been the considerable success of the Plan. They also claimed that the Plan was responsible for improving union-management and employee relations. The Plan has paid frequent bonuses.

Site 28 demonstrates the contribution of the Plan over the long term and how interest is maintained. The committee system has reinforced work-skill training, as well as training employees in solving production problems and increased leadership skills. In addition, since the Plan had aided in putting management and labor in touch with each other's goals, objectives and feelings, it serves as an excellent vehicle for introducing change into the plant and increasing the probability of acceptance. Employee participation makes employees sensitive to the problems faced by management, as well as making management more aware of employee concerns. The parties maintain a high level of commitment to the Plan's philosophy. Biannual Scanlon Plan "brainstorming" sessions are held to maintain enthusiasm for the Plan.

Because of the date of the start-up of this Scanlon Plan, and the nature of production, productivity data were not available. However, the Scanlon bonus, which may be used as a proxy for productivity, was paid in 103 of the 156 months of the plan. Table 6-7 presents the average monthly bonus.

Table 6-7
Site 28 Bonus Summary

|  | 1968 | 1969 | 1970 | 1971 | 1972 | 1973 | 1974 |
|---|---|---|---|---|---|---|---|
| Average Monthly Bonus | 5.21% | 7.03% | 17.85% | 1.23% | 12.33% | 8.62% | 17.89% |

|  | 1975 | 1976 | 1977 | 1978 | 1979 | 1980 |
|---|---|---|---|---|---|---|
| Average Monthly Bonus | 23.32% | 2.28% | 20.97% | 23.23% | 29.12% | 34.21% |

As can be seen from these results, the plan has survived two initial years of modest bonuses (5.21 percent, 7.03 percent), as well as years in which the bonus has been very meager (1.23 percent in 1971 and 2.28 percent in 1976).

Employment was analyzed for the period January 1966 - December 1981. Employment was found to be stable (t = .46, n.s.) following introduction of the Plan, with the trend unchanged (t = .15, n.s.), as well. Industry employment had a markedly downward trend. Thus employment was more stable. The grievance rate (grievances ÷ average workforce size) has declined. There have been no strikes since the Plan was introduced. Table 6-8 summarizes the performance data for all three sites.

Site 30 is a subsidiary of a large, multinational corporation. The company manufactures high-nickel alloys in two nearby plants and employs 2000 hourly and salaried employees. It is significant not only because its Scanlon Plan is 12 years old, but also because it is one of the largest Scanlon Plan firms.

The development of cooperation at both plants was largely due to union pressure. The company had for many years operated a Bedeaux individual incentive plan, covering all hourly workers. The union could contest a standard through the grievance procedure or at the next contract negotiation. However, the company made the final determination on any standard, since incentive issues were nonarbitrable.

Organized opposition to the Bedeaux Plan surfaced as early as 1957, when the union pressured management into renouncing the use of disciplinary measures against employees for failure to meet the incentive standards. They blamed it for infecting labor-management relations, claiming that it wasn't related to effort and skill, and that it had the effect of pitting worker against worker. The union leadership claimed Bedeaux led to dishonesty among the workers, as well as encouraging them to disregard quality, which often caused more work for other employees.

In 1968, the union suggested that the Bedeaux system be dropped in favor of a profit-sharing plan. The company rejected the idea, but did spend the next two years investigating a number of plantwide incentives. At that time, management found the Scanlon Plan the most suitable. The installation of a Scanlon Plan seemed even more attractive in light of a 1967 opinion survey of the company's salaried employees. These employees criticized the company's internal communications, its unresponsiveness to suggestions, and the tenuous relation between performance and incentive earnings.

## Table 6-8
## Sites 28, 30, and 9 Summary
### (Case 5)

| | Level | T-Stat | Lev Chg | T-Stat | Drift | T-Stat | Dft Chg | T-Stat |
|---|---|---|---|---|---|---|---|---|
| **Site 28** | | | | | | | | |
| Employment | 262.96 | 21.75 | 5.51 | 0.46 | 0.37 | 0.07 | 0.86 | 0.15 |
| Employment control (N = 192, df = 188) | 568.28 | 82.12 | -1.67 | -0.25 | 2.51 | 1.36 | -2.59 | -1.39 |
| Grievances (N = 79, df = 75) | 3.44 | 2.79 | 0.78 | 0.68 | -0.13 | -0.80 | 0.12 | 0.74 |
| **Site 30** | | | | | | | | |
| Productivity (N = 143, df = 139) | 27.64 | 19.82 | 1.88 | 1.35 | -0.21 | -1.09 | 0.04 | 0.22 |
| Employment | 1786.40 | 103.20 | -4.08 | -2.36** | -0.29 | -0.38 | 3.16 | 4.24+ |
| Employment control (N = 144, df = 140) | 56.63 | 35.08 | -0.50 | -0.32 | -0.23 | -0.78 | 0.23 | 0.70 |
| **Site 9** | | | | | | | | |
| Productivity | 3.80 | 19.25 | -0.39 | -1.50 | 0.00 | 0.34 | 0.01 | 0.65 |
| Employment | 122.81 | 14.22 | -6.79 | -0.76 | 1.21 | 1.68 | -0.74 | -0.62 |

$*p < .05$, $**p < .01$, $+ p < .001$

The union also conducted its own investigation of possible alternatives to Bedeaux, and concluded independently that Scanlon could meet their criteria of equity, good bonus payments for all employees, improved labor-management relations, and an opportunity for workers to make suggestions and be sure that management would listen.

In late 1970, the Plan was begun at the smaller plant which had no incentive system and was generally a much simpler operation. The company also provided the union with a letter of commitment to develop a jointly acceptable plan for the large plant. In August 1972, the Plan was adopted for a two-year trial period, with 74 percent of the hourly workers and 90 percent of the salaried employees voting in favor. Thereafter, the employees at the smaller plant voted to tie their Scanlon Plan into that of the larger plant.

This Scanlon Plan is unusual because of its large number of production committees and its three-tiered committee system.

Presently, there are 30 Production Committees, 11 Screening Committees, and a Planning and Review Committee. The Production Committees offer the greatest opportunity for employee participation. These committees, developed along departmental lines, are composed of management and employee representatives, with a management representative acting as chairperson; average membership numbers six persons. The employee representatives are elected by fellow employees in each department for staggered one-year terms, with successive terms permitted.

The Production Committees seek ways to improve their department's efficiency. The committees meet at least once a month, and are responsible for soliciting, receiving and disposing of suggestions within a reasonable time. The Production Committees can either accept or reject suggestions, or refer them to the appropriate Screening Committee. If a suggestion is accepted, the committee can institute it if the cost does not exceed $200. However, if the suggestion requires a capital purchase, the suggestion must be referred to the Engineering Screening Committee for further investigation.

When a suggestion requires an expenditure in excess of $200, or there is disagreement over it at the Production Committee level, the suggestion can be referred to the appropriate Screening Committee. Each Screening Committee represents a "group" in the plant, e.g., manufacturing, accounting, administration, etc. Every Screening Committee is chaired by a manager, with at least one employee representative for each Production Committee within a group. These committees are responsible for disposing of those suggestions referred to them. The Screening Committees can usually take action on suggestions costing more than $200 unless a capital purchase is required. These committees, which meet monthly after the bonus results are announced, also discuss the results and ways of improving bonuses, as well as ways to solve problems raised through employee participation.

The Planning and Review Committee discusses the events surrounding the monthly bonus before it is announced. The Planning and Review Committee's monthly agenda also includes comments on what helped or hurt production, business competition, monthly billings, production backlogs, and sales prospects. This committee consists of the executive vice-president (representing the president), 11 other management officials representing each group (including four from the largest group, manufacturing), the two local union presidents and eight hourly representatives from the production Screening Committees. Due to the size of the Planning and Review Committee, the employee representatives must alternate attendance in order to keep the meeting manageable. However, if a particular Production Committee is not represented at the Planning and

Review meeting, they can attend a meeting immediately following the monthly Planning and Review meeting, where the company's comptroller explains the bonus results. Finally, although the Planning and Review Committee does not normally handle suggestions, it will dispose of those which may entail great expense or effort across group lines. The Planning and Review Committee, with the approval of the vice-president of manufacturing, can authorize any non-capital expenditure up to $5,000.

Employee understanding and acceptance of the Plan was facilitated and maintained by several strategies. The company exhibited its good faith by meeting the union on its own ground before and during the Plan's operation. Management officials would travel to the union hall to answer questions and discuss problems that arose in early stages of the Plan's operation. Along with distribution of Scanlon information pamphlets, there were general meetings where union and management officials would exhibit their cohesiveness on the merits of the Plan. To maintain acceptance of the Plan, efforts are made to keep the workforce informed of the Plan's operations. Minutes are kept and made available for all Production Committee meetings. Suggestions made through these meetings receive written responses as quickly as possible. The company newsletter is utilized to maintain an awareness of the Scanlon Plan. Many articles attempt to inform the employees on the inter-relationships of the Plan and the business environment and how the Plan's performance affects the company's financial situation.

Productivity was measured by pounds per man hour for the period January 1970 - December 1981. The productivity time-series exhibited a positive upward level change ($t = 1.35$, n.s.). Over time, productivity has remained stable ($t = .22$, n.s.). Employment at Site 30 showed a statistically significant decrease in level following the intervention ($t = -2.36$, $p < .01$), while industry employment remained stable ($t = -.32$, n.s.). Over time, however, the plant experienced a highly significant upward trend in employment ($t = 4.24$, $p < .001$), while industry employment remained unchanged ($t = .70$, n.s.).

The annual number of employee suggestions has ranged from a high of 1,086 in 1973 to 227 in 1980. The employees have earned a bonus 83 percent of the time.

Site 9 is a family-owned manufacturer of steel lockers and shelves. The company employs 150 bargaining unit employees and has one of the oldest cooperative efforts in the United States.

The Scanlon Plan was first suggested by the union in 1952 during collective bargaining. No agreement could be reached and it subsequently took two years for agreement on the Plan's implementation because the company chose to move cautiously. When the Scanlon Plan was finally instituted it was to improve the relationship between the company and the union and the company and its employees; as a method for resolving problems that existed at the time; and as a financial incentive. In contrast to other Scanlon Plans of its era, this Plan was *not* begun because of economic solvency problems.

The history and philosophy of the Plan are highlighted in the employee handbook:

> While we have not earned a bonus every month since 1954, the overall record of the Scanlon Plan has been exceptional. It was originally introduced to promote further cooperation between Management and Union employees, by allowing all employees a "voice in the business." By cooperating effectively through the Scanlon Plan the . . .Company has been able to improve productivity and remain competitive with much larger producers of our type of product. Every suggestion is valuable because every employee including yourself will benefit to some degree.

Since the program at Site 9 had been in operation for 24 years, analysis of its program under the format chosen for this research would have been inappropriate. It was decided to analyze the Plan in terms of its operation and continued effectiveness. This in some respects poses interesting questions with regard to identifying the factors or variables which permit long term institutionalization of the programs. This is an important issue since it is commonly believed that cooperative programs, like the Scanlon Plan, decline over time.

There are five Production Committees organized on a departmental basis, including one each for the office and engineering, the night shift and a small facility a short distance from the main plant.

The five committees are:

1. Fabrication department
2. Painting and shipping
3. Office and engineering
4. Essex Street (small facility two blocks from main plant)
5. Night shift

Each committee has four members, three union members appointed for a term of two years and the foreman. Appointments to the Production Committee are made jointly by the union president and the personnel director on the basis of previously expressed interest as evidenced by the offering of suggestions. The Production Committees meet monthly on company time to generate and evaluate ideas. The committees have the authority to implement suggestions up to a dollar value limit of $100, as long as there is no overlap between committees. Although the Plan was more than 20 years old, during the period January 1976 - May 1979 employees made 868 suggestions and 654 (75 percent) were implemented. The annual suggestion rate was 1.5-3 suggestions per employee each year. This demonstrates that employee participation need not dissipate over time. Major areas of suggestions have come in the areas of machine die and tooling, painting methods, and paper work systems.

The Screening Committee meets twice a month also on company time. In contrast to other Scanlon Plans which tend to hold only one Screening Committee meeting per month, this firm breaks its Screening Committee functions into a short monthly meeting to discuss and evaluate the bonus and a longer meeting to review operations and business conditions. There are nine employees and four management representatives on the Screening Committee. Eight employees are selected jointly by the union president and the personnel director.

The Screening Committee tends to operate in three areas. The first is to oversee the operation of the Production Committees and to resolve any jurisdictional or cost conflicts which arise. The second is the responsibility for the management of the bonus and its allocation. Finally, the third area of operation is as a device for improved communication between the company and the union. Screening Committee discussions have centered on resolving or explaining problems and planning for potential opportunities. The company uses the Screening Committee to provide advance notice to the employees of the onset of slow periods. Also discussed are the reasons why the company may have lost a contract, areas of current production problems, and long range problems the company expects to encounter. The Screening Committee is also used as a vehicle for seizing upon opportunities. Examples of this type of usage include the exploration of better work methods and the preparation for busy periods.

The traditional Scanlon bonus formula is utilized. In a Plan that has been in place for a long period of time, periodically there is a need to review the historical relationship between labor costs and sales value of production. Technological change or a shift in the relationship between materials costs and labor costs may alter the financial basis of the Plan. The bonus is reviewed by an experienced Scanlon consultant. The consultant's neutrality, credibility and financial expertise in Plan accounting helps insure that equity is maintained.

The employees are kept informed about the Plan through several devices. All bonus reports are posted on company bulletin boards. Committee representatives provide employees with information, both through formal feedback on suggestions and ideas and informally. In addition, departmental meetings are conducted by the foremen; suggestions are interchanged across committees and are made available to anyone who is interested; and finally there is an annual dinner to honor employees who have served on the Production and Screening Committees. Because of the long term nature of the Plan, the company has developed a reputation in the community as a good place to work. This, combined with the relatively good wages paid, has enabled the company to attract better quality employees. Over the years, the company has had few hiring problems and low labor turnover. As well, the Scanlon Plan has resulted in a monthly bonus over 90 percent of the time. This stability has aided in effectuating the operation of the Plan.

Productivity and employment were analyzed for the period January 1975 - April 1979, and March 1975 - May 1979. The intervention point was the reaffirmation of the Plan by virtue of its continuation following the close of collective bargaining in Jaunary 1977. In examining Plans of long duration, it would not be expected that abrupt level changes in performance would take place. That was the case with Site 9. Productivity and employment tended to be stable, although the direction of the t-statistics for both level changes were negative. This can be explained by the severe drop in economic activity experienced by the firm through the first five months of 1977. The trend in productivity was

modestly positive (t = -.65, n.s.) while the trend in employment was slightly downward (t = -.62, n.s.).

These three sites demonstrate that long term cooperation
is possible. Site 30 shows that it can occur in a large,
multiplant environment. Site 28 shows that the Scanlon Plan
has the capability of serving as the centerpiece of an
organization's human resource management efforts. Site 9
proves that the plan has the capability of enduring very long
periods of time (30 years).

What conditions were present? First, the Scanlon Plan was
suggested by the trade unions, indicating the support that the
Plan, originally developed by the United Steel Workers, en-
joys among some unionists. Management also investigated
and determined that the Plan would fit into the culture of the
organization. The Plans have been successful in moving decisionmaking down to the shop floor and the commitment to
employee involvement has not been breached. In all three
sites, extensive efforts are made to keep workers and
managers informed. Finally, all three plans, while not paying
bonuses every month, have consistently done so.

## Case Study 6: The Failure to Maintain Equity

Sites 5 (450 hourly employees) and 7 (250 hourly
employees) are plants within the same division of a large industrial conglomerate. The plants manufacture different
types of chain, are geographically separated by 45 miles,
have distinct sets of managers, and are represented by different locals of the same international union who bargain
separate collective bargaining agreements. At the same time,
however, there were some common features associated with
the initiation and operation of the Plans which can be
presented simultaneously.

Eight years prior to the institution of the Rucker Plan, the
company and the unions had agreed to eliminate the plants'

incentive systems. During the 1970s, both plants were being adversely affected by foreign competition. The Rucker Plan was introduced to improve productivity (and the firm's competitive position), to provide additional earnings for employees' efforts (the company had taken a firm stance in bargaining with the union on wages), and to improve communications.

The overall structure of the two Rucker Plans was the same. Each had a suggestion system, two employee committees, and a bonus formula. In the Rucker Plan setting, employees submit suggestions to an Idea Coordinator. The Idea Coordinator pursues the suggestion with appropriate managerial personnel and feeds back a response to the employee.

The employee committees are divided into Production and Steering. The Production Committees primarily consist of rank-and-file workers; they review all suggestions (accepted and rejected) and discuss such problem areas in the plant as quality, materials and pricing. At Site 5 employees were elected to serve on the committee for three-month periods, whereas at Site 7, employees were chosen by management with the approval of the union for six-month intervals. The Screening Committees, composed of top union and company officials, addressed questions similar to those above, but also considered more significant matters. Some of these involved marketplace and general economic considerations, pricing decisions, product design, the introduction of new products, and the bonus calculations.

The bonus formula is based on the relationship between bargaining unit payroll costs and production value. Production value is calculated by subtracting defective goods returned and the costs of materials, supplies, and services from the sale value of goods sold. At Site 5 this relationship was determined to be 37.74 percent while at Site 7 it was 40.91 percent. Although there were substantial increases in productivity, at both sites few bonuses were paid. This was due to a divisional management decision not to raise prices. At a time of rapidly rising costs for materials, supplies, and services, this decision eliminated most of the potential bonus. Table 6-9 summarizes the performance for both sites.

The productivity (output per hour) and employment data for Site 5 were analyzed for the periods January 1975 - October 1978 and January 1974 - December 1978, respectively. The intervention point was July 1976, the introduction of the Rucker Plan. The results indicate that employment was unchanged ($t = .58$, n.s.) while the industry was slightly downward. The more interesting finding is that the level of productivity increased ($t = 2.30$, $p < .05$), but that the trend was negative ($t = -2.53$, $p < .01$). This would indicate that the plan had had an initial positive effect, which had dissipated rather quickly. In 1976, there were three bonus months (13.2, 28.6, and 37.4 cents per hour). For three years (1977-79), only one monthly bonus was paid (2.56 cents per hour).

At Site 7, productivity (output per hour) and employment were analyzed for the period January 1974 - October 1978 and January 1974 - March 1979, respectively, with the intervention point being July 1976. The productivity improvement that occurred was quite pronounced. There was an abrupt upward shift in the level of productivity ($t = 4.99$, $p < .001$) followed by a stable trend ($t = 0.14$, n.s.). This is shown in figure 6-4. Employment was unchanged following introduction of the Rucker Plan, but a downward trend prior to the intervention was reversed, following a pattern similar to the industry.

At this site bonuses were larger, but were not paid regularly. In 1976, no bonuses were paid; in 1977, there were two bonus months of 14.8 cents and 56.8 cents per hour; in 1978, two bonuses of 46.8 cents and 33.4 cents per hour with a 2.79 cents per hour end-of-the-year bonus were paid.

Table 6-9
Sites 5 and 7 Summary
(Case 6)

| | Level | T-Stat | Lev Chg | T-Stat | Drift | T-Stat | Dft Chg | T-Stat |
|---|---|---|---|---|---|---|---|---|
| **Site 5** | | | | | | | | |
| Productivity (N = 46, df = 42) | 12.91 | 18.74 | 1.94 | 2.30* | 0.05 | 0.85 | -0.18 | -2.53** |
| Employment (N = 60, df = 56) | 624.72 | 28.97 | 12.58 | 0.58 | -6.21 | -1.35 | 8.52 | 1.31 |
| **Site 7** | | | | | | | | |
| Productivity (N = 58, df = 54) | 3.37 | 24.16 | 0.98 | 4.99+ | 0.01 | 0.66 | 0.00 | 0.14 |
| Employment (N = 55, df = 51) | 413.67 | 46.74 | 8.46 | 0.96 | -3.91 | -1.91 | 2.43 | 0.98 |

**p<.01, +p<.001

**Figure 6-4**
**Site 7 Productivity**

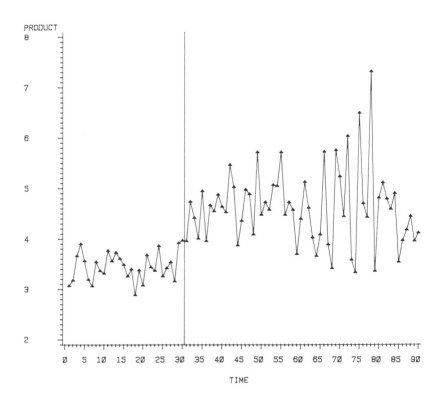

At both sites, the suggestion programs, which had initially been quite active, experienced steady decline and became mostly inactive. Finally, just prior to the three-year anniversary of the Rucker Plan, a four-month strike took place during the renegotiation of the collective bargaining agreement. The failure of the Plan to pay consistent bonuses was a key factor in this prolonged strike.

A question arises as to why productivity increased, but a bonus was not paid. In order to understand this, the Rucker bonus formula must be re-examined. The formula is

Sales Value of Production
- Costs of Goods Sold (materials, supplies)

PRODUCTION VALUE
x Labor Ratio

Allowed Payroll

to establish the existence and size of the bonus pool. Ideally, the price of the product, as well as the prices paid for materials and supplies, and labor costs should move in the same pattern as they had in the base period, normally two-five years prior to the plan. Any deviation in this pattern can lessen a bonus earned or possibly create a bonus when one was not deserved. In the case of the two plants, there was an increase in volume of production, thus raising the sales value of production. However, because the price of the product remained constant, the growth was not as large as it would have been with a price increase. More important, there were sharp increases in material costs, energy, and other items used in production. Payroll also increased due to negotiated wage increases, the quarterly cost of living adjustment, health care cost increases, and other "roll-up costs." All of these cost factors combined to offset productivity and volume gains to eliminate much of the potential bonus.

This result is not unique to the Rucker measurement system. It is theoretically possible with the Scanlon Plan as well. With an Improshare Plan, the bonus is based on engineered time standards and actual hours of work. Therefore, shifts in the price of production, costs of goods sold, and labor costs have no bearing on the bonus.

In the Kochan-Dyer model of organizational change in unionized settings, an important factor in institutionalizing union-management cooperation over time is the equitable distribution of benefits stemming from the endeavor. Equity was not present in this situation. At the outset, the Rucker Plan was strongly supported by the employees at both sites. However, as a result of the failure to pay a bonus, interest had lessened. A good indication of this was the decline in the suggestion program. At Site 5, the decline in productivity which occurred, after an initial significant improvement would appear to lend support to the Kochan-Dyer theory.

Of greater concern, however, is the lack of control workers have concerning their earnings in these group productivity-sharing plans. This problem is not limited solely to Rucker Plans. Herein are two cases in which worker productivity has increased, yet additional earnings have not been forthcoming. Management's ability to affect the bonus in a nonmanipulative manner highlights the fact that workers may not be in control of their destinies in these situations.

## Case Study 7: A Failure to Match the Labor-Management Relationship With the Intervention

Site 6 manufactured steel casters and wheels and employed 129 hourly personnel. The Scanlon Plan resulted from compromises made by the company in collective bargaining with the union. The company had proposed the institution of an individual incentive system. The union rejected this proposal and alternately proposed the development of a Scanlon Plan. Although the company preferred a different group incentive plan, at the union's insistence it agreed to the Scanlon Plan.

The Plan followed the traditional Scanlon design with a suggestion system, four Production Committees, and one Screening Committee. The bonus formula included both hourly, clerical, and salaried employees. An analysis of the minutes of Screening Committee meetings indicated that most of its deliberations involved discussing suggestions sent to it by the Production Committees. In contrast to other

Scanlon Plans studied, there was almost no discussion of long range and environmental issues.

A bonus was paid in 9 (4.8 percent), 10 (3.4 percent), and 2 (0.02 percent) of the 13 (annual) possible bonus periods in the three years of the Plan's existence. Only in the first year was there an end-of-the-year surplus in the reserve (5.5 percent). In the last year (1979), the Plan paid only one bonus of 2.5 percent (February).

In July 1979 management unilaterally withdrew the office and salaried groups from the calculation of the bonus claiming that any bonus that was being earned was the result of efforts by those groups. This raised the specter of bonus formula manipulation, and following six more bonus periods without positive results, the union exercised its right to terminate upon 30 days notice, thus ending the Plan.

The productivity and employment experience for Site 6 was analyzed for the period January 1975 - December 1979 and January 1974 - December 1979, respectively, with the intervention occurring in December 1976. There was a positive, although not statistically significant increase in productivity ($t = 1.47$, n.s.) following the introduction of the Plan. Over time, a downward drift in productivity was reversed and shifted upward ($t = 2.35$, $p < .05$). Employment remained unchanged ($t = -0.59$, n.s.) and tended to follow an upward industry pattern. These results are summarized in table 6-10.

Table 6-10
Site 6 Summary
(Case 7)

|  | Level | T-Stat | Lev Chg | T-Stat |
|---|---|---|---|---|
| Productivity (N = 54, df = 50) | 64.25 | 19.28 | 6.20 | 1.47 |

|  | Drift | T-Stat | Dft Chg | T-Stat |
|---|---|---|---|---|
|  | -0.35 | -1.43 | .68 | 2.35* |

|  | Level | T-Stat | Lev Chg | T-Stat |
|---|---|---|---|---|
| Employment (N = 50, df = 46) | 96.95 | 15.69 | -3.61 | -0.59 |

|  | Drift | T-Stat | Dft Chg | T-Stat |
|---|---|---|---|---|
|  | 2.97 | 2.40 | -0.52 | -0.31 |

*p < .05

The Scanlon Plan at Site 6 appears to have been moderately successful in improving productivity. The demise of the Plan after three years exemplifies the effects of deviation from Scanlon Plan theory. First, the Scanlon Plan is much more than an incentive system. It is a different philosophy of conducting an organization's operations. This aspect of the Plan was missing here. Decisionmaking authority was never truly placed in the hands of the Production Committees. Approximately 40 percent of the Production Committee suggestions were referred to the Screening Committee. The Screening Committee never became a vehicle for higher level communication between the company and the union. Contrary to the Scanlon philosophy that the entire organization works together, the separation of the office and salaried workforce from the bonus formula is additional evidence that this management had not completely accepted the full basis of the Plan. Finally, adjustment of the bonus in midyear, for factors other than extensive technological or financial reasons, seriously imperiled the requisite sense of organizational equity needed to facilitate the cooperative process.

The Scanlon Plan is not an appropriate intervention when the motives of the partisans are solely to replace an out-of-date individual incentive system with a plantwide bonus plan. Nor is the Plan likely to be successful when used as a mechanism to replace lost earnings resulting from a concession bargaining agreement or wage moratorium. This Scanlon Plan was installed into a labor-management relationship in which the philosophy of management did not fit the values inherent in the Scanlon philosophy.

## Case Study 8: The Failure of Cooperation to Take Hold

Site 2 manufactures carburetors for automobiles and farm machinery and electromagnetic clutches for business machines, mail sorting equipment and for farm and industrial machinery. In 1966, the plant employed 1700 people and was the major employer in the community. Shortly thereafter, the company lost its tariff protection and began to be adversely affected by foreign competition in its major product line. This pressure caused the company to move production of that product line out of the country. The move resulted in a 25 percent reduction in the plant's business and a loss of 700 jobs.

The major loss of jobs and further potential economic threats in the highly competitive automotive components industry led the parties to begin a series of informal discussions concerning future economic conditions and what solutions might be possible. As a result of top management pressure, a special meeting between the company and union's nine-member bargaining committee was held in June 1972.

The union asked the company what was needed to insure the plant's economic viability. The company responded that it needed a wage cut. From June 1972 - November 1972 negotiations began on a company proposal for a wage reduction. In November 1972, agreement was reached on a moratorium on all wage increases. This lasted for one year. In addition, the company and the union agreed to create a Joint Management-Labor Study Committee (JM-LSC). The Study Committee's mission was incorporated into the collective bargaining agreement as a memorandum of understanding. The agreement stated that the goal of the JM-LSC was

> . . . to investigate solutions to productivity and employee utilization problems. The responsibility of the Committee is to study and evaluate such problems and *recommend* solutions (emphasis added by editor).[5]

The JM-LSC consisted of six members (three union and three management) and would meet on an as-needed basis. The Committee participants were:

| Union | Management |
|---|---|
| 1. union president | 1. manager of industrial relations |
| 2. union committeeman | 2. director of manufacturing |
| 3. hourly employee | 3. manager of manufacturing engineering |

The parties stated that the philosophy of the cooperative effort was

> . . . that only through a constructive new approach to productivity and employee utilization problems can they (the parties) achieve a competitive operation, offering good employment opportunity with a reasonable expectation of job security.[6]

Although a part of the plant's difficulty stemmed from an antiquated incentive system, a far more serious problem occurred when corporate management provided a wage increase for the salaried staff shortly after plant management and the union had agreed to the wage moratorium. In spite of strong objections by the plant manager, the corporation instituted a 5 percent wage increase for the salaried employees. According to the personnel manager, the action by the corporation clouded the developing cooperative relationship between the company and the union. He further stated that it was his belief that the subsequent ineffectiveness of the JM-LSC, was in large part the result of the distrust generated by this action.

Analysis of the minutes of the JM-LSC meetings and interview data indicate that the committee operated in several areas. The JM-LSC considered matters related to work scheduling, overall staffing requirements, job classifications, full utilization of employees, and general business conditions. At the committee's initial meeting (January 10, 1973) eight areas of productivity improvement were identified. Minutes of the meeting indicate that some of the areas were employee centered items while others dealt with more efficient management of operations. The employee centered areas appear to demonstrate a general belief on the part of management that some of the firm's economic problems were related to employee attitudes and behavior. Management referred to the problems of late starts and early quits, absenteeism, and abuses of breaks and rest periods. The areas identified for managerial improvement were: utilization of manpower and equipment, utilization of service and skill trades manpower, creation of new incentives, and production procedures including methods to reduce downtime.

During the initial meetings, the company and the union worked to improve communication between the parties and with the employees. The minutes indicated that the parties held a "broad and general discussion" on the areas identified for productivity improvement. At the union's suggestion, management sent letters to its employees which outlined the current business prospects and made reference to productivity needs. This was followed two months later by an additional letter which discussed the introduction of a new product line.

The JM-LSC identified difficulties related to poor management. For example, in a discussion of excessive downtime it was pointed out that this was the result of shortages of purchased parts, lack of tooling, and removal of produced parts. These shortages made it most difficult to keep work ahead of the employees or to permit them to be kept active for an entire shift. This according to the committee resulted in overtime work at the end of the month.

The union also made several suggestions which management rejected. The first was a union proposal to put nonincentive jobs in a key section on to the incentive system. This was put under investigation, and after a detailed study no decision was made to make the change. In another instance, the union suggested, but the corporation opposed, a large capital expenditure to permit the purchase of machinery, equipment and tooling to permit expansion into a recently developed market.

From the initial meeting, one of the goals of the plant's management was to change work habits and patterns. In this regard, the union leadership appeared willing at the outset to assist. In a discussion of absuse of the rest period the committee concluded that "the most logical solution to the problem is a more conscious awareness in enforcing it on the floor."

Thereafter, the parties addressed the issue of "pegged performance" on incentive jobs. They agreed to a joint program of supervisory and employee meetings to explain the nature of the problems besetting the plant and to request employee cooperation in doing away with pegged production.

Shortly thereafter, the union's cooperative attitude seems to have lessened as a result of major layoff. On June 20, 1973, the union informed the company that it should not expect improved productivity when "disturbances are created by a removal of the majority of the third shift. . . ." At the same time, the union complained that several other areas of the plant were working regular overtime which they claimed caused absenteeism and a decline in individual productivity. The union further stated that there were limited opportunities for increased production due to employees being on short work weeks. Finally, the union pointed to management ineffectiveness, e.g., the delay in getting tools and stock and the movement of completed stock. Thereafter, when the company raised the absenteeism problem and a sudden decline in productivity, the union stressed the short term recall and layoff, short work weeks, lack of materials or parts, and excessive tool problems.

At one point, the company committeemen proposed a reclassification of a position from one department to another at the same rate of pay. The company claimed the proposed change was needed because of its inability to provide a full day's work due to the variance in set-up times. The union committeemen took the position that the subject was an inappropriate one for the Productivity Committee and one better suited for the Bargaining Committee. They further stated that in principle they saw no need for change.

At this point of the committee's experience, a crucial stage was reached. The corporation had authorized the purchase of new cost savings equipment. The company reminded the union of the need for normal work effort by operators during time studies to establish production standards, and the need for a proper attitude by the operators in order to protect operators from loss of normal earnings. In addition, this would have permitted the division to demonstrate its ability to meet its goals and targets. However, within a month thereafter, the union was to complain of a lack of employee confidence in the setting of new rates for the newly purchased machinery.

As the JM-LSC progressed through the summer of 1974, it became apparent that there was a great deal of redundancy in the issues discussed. The company continued to discuss its problems with absenteeism, while at the same time, the union continued to stress difficulties caused by management personnel. There is no doubt that the initial meetings of the JM-LSC were helpful in highlighting issues for future development. However, the level of action taken to develop ideas and programs for the resolution of productivity problems never occurred.

The parties at this plant were never able to reach a truly cooperative stage. In addition to the problems created by the salaried employees' pay increase and third shift layoff, several other factors may help explain the absence of cooperation. First, the members of the JM-LSC were for the most part the same individuals who regularly negotiated contracts and settled grievances. The tone and conduct of the meetings were reported to be representative of that which took place at the bargaining table. In contrast to most labor-management committees the plant manager never took part in the committee's deliberations.

A second factor appears to be the inability of the parties to reach a stage beyond that of the union placing the blame for productivity difficulties on management, and vice-versa. If the parties had been able to resolve or show progress on even a minor problem, perhaps a more cooperative shift would have been engendered. Related to this seems to be the animosity toward hourly employees held by the management. In other companies investigated for this study, more progressive management policies tended to produce more responsible behavior on the part of the employees. In this particular case, the management response to dysfunctional employee attitudes and behaviors was a "hard-nosed" desire to "enforce the rules."

Finally, job security became an over-riding issue for the union and its members. There were recurrent rumors that additional production would be moved overseas. Management was never successful in dispelling these rumors.

During 1973, the JM-LSC met 12 times. In 1974 the number of meetings totaled only six. In the minutes of the last several meetings it is clear that very little was being accomplished due to one side or the other rejecting its counterpart's proposals. Following the last meeting, both the company and the union mutually agreed to allow the committee to die out with the caveat that they would meet again if either side felt that there was something to discuss. Although the JM-LSC continues to be part of the collective bargaining agreement, neither side has called a meeting in nearly 10 years.

Site 2 was only willing to provide employment data. The employment experience does demonstrate the severity of the problems faced by this plant and the strength of the stimulus for cooperation. The employment data were analyzed for the period November 1970 - October 1974 with the intervention point being the start of the JM-LSC, November 1972. As shown in table 6-11, there was a statistically significant reduction in employment following the start-up of the committee ($t = -8.59$, $p < .001$). Moreover, in contrast to other sites in the study, Site 2's experience was dramatically different from the industry at large. Figure 6-5 demonstrates that as the plant's employment was falling sharply, there was an industry-wide steady upward trend.

Table 6-11
Site 2 Summary
(Case 8)

|  | Level | T-Stat | Lev Chg | T-Stat |
|---|---|---|---|---|
| Employment (N = 48, df = 44) | 576.08 | 37.65 | -170.97 | -8.59+ |

|  | Drift | T-Stat | Dft Chg | T-Stat |
|---|---|---|---|---|
|  | 9.65 | 9.44 | -17.59 | -12.15+ |

+ p < .001

This site demonstrates that a strong stimulus for change, i.e., loss of jobs and a further potential reduction in employment was not enough for cooperation to be successful. Moreover, creating a cooperative structure without a change of attitude among the principals will not result in meaningful labor-management cooperation. It is clear that neither labor nor management demonstrated a sufficient degree of trust or candor to permit the type of problemsolving interaction to truly resolve the significant problems facing the company. The behavior of the participants seemed to closely parallel that which would be expected in actual collective bargaining. An expanded committee membership might have alleviated this.

The JM-LSC might have been more effective had a neutral been involved. Other plant committees have benefitted from third party involvement, particularly when provided by an Area Labor-Management Committee. The neutral might have been able to set up a more problemsolving oriented commitee structure and procedure. The presence of a neutral might have permitted a more open exchange of views and the neutral might have offered his/her own ideas to improve the parties' relationship.

**Figure 6-5**
**Site 2 Employment**

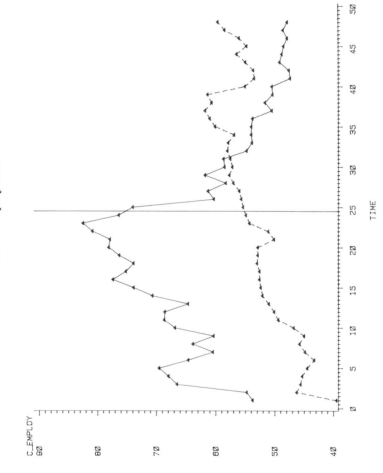

Finally, it was not possible to buffer the cooperative process from other workplace issues. The pay raise for salaried employees, the layoffs of additional workers, and the reduction in hours for others made commitment by the union leadership difficult and led the union participants to take hard-line positions on many issues.

## Case Study 9: Mixing QWL Concepts with Traditional Union-Management Issues

Site 3 manufactures ball bearings and at the time of this research had 699 production employees. Labor relations at this plant have been mixed. Prior to 1969, there were several small walkouts. From 1969-1974, relations were quite peaceful. The 1974 contract negotiations resulted in a two-week strike, while the 1977 contract was settled peacefully.

In 1973, the division's business declined and 200 jobs were moved from the plant to a facility in the South. At that point, the union agreed to the creation of a joint in-plant committee, but only assigned lesser ranking officials to it. The company assigned the works manager (plant manager) and the personnel director. The committee had met for three months when an in-plant dispute occurred which resulted in an end to the cooperative relationship.

In 1975, the plant needed to make changes in order to insure its economic survival. There had been a severe layoff and 300 of the plant's 800 jobs were moved to the southern plant. The union president who was said to be committed to the quality of worklife concept raised the idea of a cooperative labor-management program with his constituents. In December 1975, at a general membership meeting, the rank-and-file voted to approve the creation of a six-member (three union/three management) Union-Management Study Group on Productivity and Quality of Worklife. One proviso was that any agreement that was reached had to be brought back to the membership for their approval.

The company chose the works manager, manufacturing manager, and personnel and industrial relations manager to serve on the committee, while representing the union were the local president, chairman of the office bargaining unit, and one committeeman from the factory. The Study Group was defined as

> . . . a joint effort by the Union and Company to explore new ideas and better ways of doing things for the benefit of both the employees and the company by using the natural resources of the plant employees, both Union and Management in a voluntary way sharing gains jointly.[7]

The Study Group had no decisionmaking authority, but could make recommendations compatible with the Group's mission, which covered four areas:

(1) Productivity Improvement
(2) Quality of Worklife
(3) Reward/Pay Systems
(4) Human Relations

> To develop relations that encourage teamwork and understanding between people . . . to provide an honest, open communication system that promotes a sense of responsibility, pride, satisfaction, and recognition for achievement.

The Study Group's first meeting was held on January 29, 1976. At that time, agreement was reached that the group should not focus on union-management distinctions, but instead each committee member should be free to discuss ideas freely and openly.

The Group also decided to utilize outside consultants. The consultants offered several ideas including the elimination of status symbols, the use of people to generate "on the floor ideas" and the creation of a formalized system of communication.

From the beginning, the Study Group decided to formally communicate with the rank-and-file. The Study Group met with groups of 40 employees (management and union) for one hour on company time. Each member of the Study Group was assigned a specific QWL issue to discuss, with sufficient time permitted to allow employees to ask questions. At the end of the meetings, each employee was asked to write down what they liked or disliked about each area of discussion. The Study Group concluded that the biggest fear the employees had was job security. Finally, the Study Group met with the foremen and stewards, since the Group believed they were an important communications link to the employees.

Minutes of the Study Group's meeting of March 4, 1976, indicate that an experimental work redesign project was rejected by the employees involved. The department had voted to reject a team approach. The minutes of the Study Group offer a valuable lesson.

> Everyone agreed that the issue was one of security and not with the team concept itself . . . everyone agreed it was necessary to let the responsibility and the vote rest with the turning teams as responsible adults.

Thereafter the Study Group formed seven plant subcommittees of 6-12 persons, all volunteers. These committees met for one hour, two times per week, for three weeks to develop ideas for their immediate work areas. The subcommittee chairpersons received in-house team building training while the subcomittee members, stewards, and supervisors were briefed on the expected operation of the subcommittees.

Problems arose in the subcommittees. Several chairpersons resigned because of pressures brought by the people in their areas. In addition, the skilled trades group dropped out and soon thereafter, the first member of the Study Group resigned, also as the result of pressures from shop floor.

The Joint Study Group visited other firms, at company expense, to gain ideas and exposure to other cooperative ventures.

After six months the efforts of the Joint Study Group resulted in the following changes:

(1) Elimination of assigned parking
(2) Addition of piped-in music on the shop floor
(3) Installation of clocks on the walls

These minimal changes upset office and staff personnel who felt that their status had been reduced in the process. As a result, the office bargaining unit successfully negotiated for the reinstitution of assigned parking. It was reported that the supervisory staff were also sympathetic to the issues raised by the office unit.

The Study Group completed its work in early 1977. The final product of the group's efforts, dated March 8, 1977, was an agreement known as the *Experimental Quality of Work Life Program* (EQWLP).

The *Experimental Quality of Work Life Program* pledged the company and the union to work towards the following goals:

(1)   To make jobs more meaningful and work more satisfying for employees, salaried and hourly, by encouraging concepts which allow for direct input by employees, thus promoting teamwork, responsibility, trust, pride, satisfaction and recognition of achievement.

(2) The development of a program that will work towards improved productivity, and if increased productivity results ways of rewarding employees by sharing the benefits of increased productivity will become legitimate matters for inclusion in the program.

Thus, in spite of previous opposition, the Study Group recommended a program that would contain elements such as shop floor committees, job redesign, autonomous work groups and gainsharing. Employee participation in the program was to be voluntary. The decision to participate was to be made within designed work groups, with the final decision determined by majority rule. After "a fair trial period" any group would have been permitted to terminate its program, once again by a vote. It should be pointed out that the company would have been permitted to terminate a group with 30 days notice.

The EQWLP provided for significant job protection and income security provisions. The job protection language was explicit.

No worker or groups of workers will lose pay or seniority or be laid off from the plant as a direct result of this quality of work life experiment conducted in the plant whether they are a participant or not.

The company and the union also agreed that an equitable means would be found to adjust for employees whose jobs would have been made unnecessary or "surplused" as a result of the program. An exception to the employment security provisions was made for jobs lost as a result of adverse business conditions or technological change.

The parties agreed that for each work group that implemented the EQWLP, a method of wage payment be found that would provide for ". . . earnings equivalent to those previously enjoyed or greater." The provisions of the collective bargaining agreement were protected. No activities under the program would have been permitted to "contravene, change, or otherwise affect any provisions of the current collective bargaining agreements . . ." without prior approval of each party. Each party was given the right to terminate the EQWLP program upon 60 days notice. If this occurred, any provisions previously agreed to would have been "contravened," and the pre-program and status quo reestablished. Any workplace changes that might have been made unilaterally by the company under the collective bargaining agreement would be permitted to remain in force at the discretion of the management.

The company agreed to pay the principal costs of the program. These included (1) provisions for group meetings; (2) the services of expert consultants (jointly chosen); (3) the conduct of employee meetings on company time; (4) the costs of new training programs; and (5) the costs of providing company information deemed necessary by the Joint Study Group.

The Joint Study Group was to oversee the operation of the EQWLP. It was to have been a ten-member panel (five union and five management members). The union members were specified under the agreement as being the

(1) union president;
(2) chairman of the office bargaining committee;
(3) chairman of the factor bargaining committee; and
(4) two other elected union officials selected by the union president.

The Joint Study Group was empowered to designate other working committees to develop methods for problem resolution, and to develop additional communication programs to further the objectives of the EQWLP. Finally, provisions were made to amend the program by mutual agreement.

The EQWLP was defeated by a vote of the union's membership—129 in favor, 540 opposed. Three factors help to explain the outcome. First, there was a split on the union negotiating committee. The local president and several members of the bargaining committee were not in agreement on the merits of the program. Negotiating committee members were not directly involved in the development of the EQWLP and there was on-going opposition by various groups of workers which tended to influence some committee members. Second, the EQWLP became intertwined in internal union politics. The vote on the program came shortly before a union election and the opposition used the program as a political issue against people who had worked to develop the EQWLP. Third, the union reported that many supervisors, roughly 50 percent of whom had come from the bargaining unit, had opposed the program. Supervisors feared their jobs would be threatened, and it may be that their subtle opposition convinced many employees to oppose the program.

The management reported that it had done a poor job selling the program to supervision, office employees, and the rank-and-file. Convincing arguments on the need for this type of change were lacking. It was never made clear why this particular strategy was selected. It should also be noted that the stimulus for change, a difficult economic recession, had begun to subside. The job security provisions may not have convinced a skeptical workforce that had already seen a sizable number of employees lose their jobs to a nonunion southern plant that the remaining jobs would be preserved.

Finally, both sides placed considerable responsibility for the program's failure on the consultants. According to committee minutes, both sides seemed to feel that the corporate consultant and one of the academic consultants were pushing them too fast and that this was causing a great deal of stress.

It was felt that the consultants were not sufficiently experienced in labor relations, nor did they fully understand the internal operations of unions. Evidence that the process was moving too fast and was facing demise included: the initial defeats of an experimental project, the resignation of a union steering committee member, and other indicators of shop floor opposition that the change process was moving faster than political support within the union.

The operation of the program had the potential of offsetting hard won contract rights. A majority vote of a work group would be needed to implement a change effort. This created uncertainty. For example, the collective bargaining agreement provided for job assignments based on seniority. There was no guarantee that individual worker job rights would be preserved if a majority of a work group voted for change. There was a fear that people at different pay grades would be doing the same job. Other workers feared a loss of earnings if the individual incentive system were eliminated, in spite of guarantees to the contrary.

This cooperative effort failed for several reasons. There was a dispute among the union's leadership as to the merits of the program, one leader having resigned from the committee. Kochan and Dyer have suggested that if coalitions develop to block the cooperative venture, gaining an initial commitment will be less likely. The evidence from this case strongly supports this contention as opposition surfaced from several groups including union members of the committee, supervision, and the office bargaining unit. Second, workers were very sensitive to job security issues and will be very resistant to change unless this important issue is addressed in a meaningful way. Third, the process of change may have moved too quickly, particularly in view of the opposition. It may take more than a well-meaning committee to reduce years of distrust. Finally, the stimulus for change (the recession) subsided with improved economic conditions. Again, Kochan and Dyer posit that if the stimulus for change lessens, so will the party's desire for change.

## Case Study 10: The Misuse of Gainsharing

This case represents the misuse of gainsharing. The plant was composed of four separate operating divisions of a large multinational manufacturing corporation. Site 12 (250 indirect employees)[8] manufactured gas compressors; Site 13 (95 indirect employees) manufactured air compressors; Site 14 (20 indirect employees) manufactured small compressors; and Site 15 (23 indirect employees) manufactured valves and regulators. Each division was an independent profit center, with the division managers reporting to different corporate vice-presidents. In spite of the management structure, there was only one union representing all the employees and a single collective bargaining agreement. There was a centralized industrial relations function. In contrast to other companies in this situation, however, there was no single actor on site with the authority to settle differences of opinion among the division managers.

As a very traditional manufacturing firm, the company was highly committed to individual incentive systems. Most of the direct labor employees were on Halsey, Rowan, or other individual incentives. Indirect workers were paid hourly wages and thus had significantly lower earnings than incentive employees. In contract negotiations, the union made a strong case for upgrading the pay of indirect employees, and management made a commitment to raise the wages of this group. Rather than a direct pay increase, management proposed, and the union agreed to an Improshare Plan. The expectation of the company was that the Improshare Plan would help increase employee performance to offset the pay increase.

Because of differences in the nature of production, style of management, and management preferences in the four operating divisions, there were four Improshare Plans. Each Plan was composed solely of indirect employees, but the

Plans were similar in that they were composed of the same types of employees (e.g., material handlers) who had previously received the same wages. *The Plans differed in their accounting procedures and plan standard (called Base Productivity Factor).* In most incentive plans, individual, group, or plantwide, there is a fairly direct relationship between performance and reward. However, for these groups of indirect employees the relationship between effort and reward was very tenuous. The individual worker was never able to see how his/her efforts related to the earning of a bonus. Factors such as the level of business activity and the efforts by the direct labor force were more likely to influence the earning of a bonus.

The site utilized two operating committees. The most active was the Division Committee, which met on a monthly basis. This committee was comprised of the following members: the personnel manager; the operations manager and the manufacturing manager; one financial analyst and one industrial engineer from each division; the union time study observer; two bargaining unit members; and the union president. There were no provisions in the plans which stated the committee's purpose, scope, or authoritative power.

The committee meetings were generally used to discuss operational problems. For example, when work was subcontracted between groups, the committee had to decide how to account for the effected group's earned hours. The Committee also monitored the bonus percentages of the groups. This might involve comparing the current bonuses with previous figures or evaluating various factors that impacted on the bonuses.

The union president stated that the meetings were basically a "gripe session." Methods, ideas, and/or suggestions relating to productivity improvement were never discussed. There was general agreement between all of the interviewees that the sessions were generally "facts and figures" meetings; there was never any constructive discussion of productivity issues.

The other operating committee, designed to handle large group matters and major problems was the Ad Hoc Committee. The membership of this committee included: the group operations managers, an internal consultant manufacturing engineer manager, the director of industrial relations, the union president, and the Grievance Committee. The Ad Hoc Committee was very active in the developmental stages of the plans. Thereafter, it would only convene if a major revision was required, such as a change in the time standard, or possibly the Base Productivity Factor.

Thus, the Improshare Plan did not provide for employee participation. There was no orientation program to acquaint employees with the operation of the Plan, nor were there Plan documents or an employee handbook to explain the operation of the bonus formula. This was unfortunate since of the three gainsharing plans—Scanlon, Rucker, and Improshare—the Improshare bonus formula is the most complex and difficult for employees (as well as managers) to understand.

Productivity at Site 12 was measured as the ratio of adjusted (constant) labor dollars shipped[9] and indirect hours charged during the period July 1976 - June 1982. Productivity at Sites 13, 14 and 15 was measured by establishing a relationship between direct employee labor hours ÷ indirect employee labor hours worked for the period January 1977 - July 1982. It was not possible to utilize an output per hour measure due to the nature of production and limitation in the management information system.

This second measure, while not optimal, was an attempt to estimate the productivity of only the indirect employees. If productivity of the indirect workers increased, it would require fewer hours to service the direct employees. The intervention point was the introduction of the Improshare Plan in August 1979.

Employment at Site 12 was measured for the period January 1976 - June 1982, while at the other three it was analyzed for the period January 1979 - June 1982. The relationship between the number of indirect employees and direct employees at Site 12 was also measured as a ratio for the period January 1976 - June 1982. Table 6-12 summarizes the statistical analysis of this data and figure 6-6 provides a visual examination of the productivity data.

Productivity at Site 12 was unchanged throughout the productivity time-series for both level and drift ($t = -.41$ and $-.32$, respectively, both n.s.). Employment was unchanged following the Plan's introduction ($t = .18$, n.s.). Over time, the division's employment was stable ($t = -.38$, n.s.), while the industry showed a downward trend ($t = -1.33$, n.s.). The relationship between the employment levels of indirect and direct workers remained unchanged throughout the time-series ($t = .10$ and $-.68$, n.s.).

Productivity at Site 13 remained initially stable following the intervention ($t = .32$, n.s.). Over time, however, productivity showed a statistically significant downward trend ($t = -3.39$, $p < .001$) (see figure 6-7). There was a statistically significant increase in the level of employment ($t = 2.12$, $p < .05$), while the industry suffered a downturn ($t = -1.00$, n.s.). The trend for both the division ($t = -.56$, n.s.) and industry employment ($t = -.85$, n.s.) remained stable.

Site 14's productivity time-series exhibited a downward level change following the Plan's introduction ($t = -1.11$, n.s.) and was generally stable over time ($t = -.88$, n.s.). The division's employment level and trend were stable over the time-series ($t = .77$ and $t = .79$, both n.s.). Industry employment, however, decreased following the intervention

**Figure 6-6**
**Site 12 Productivity**

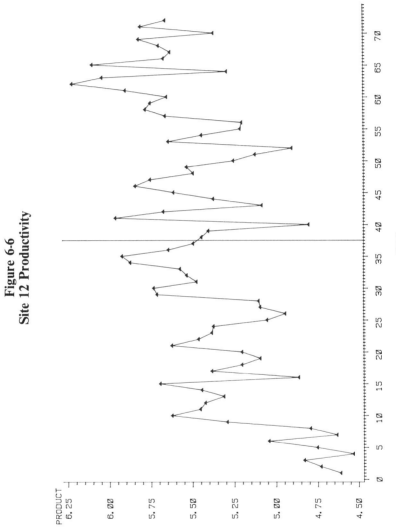

**Figure 6-7**
**Site 13 Productivity**

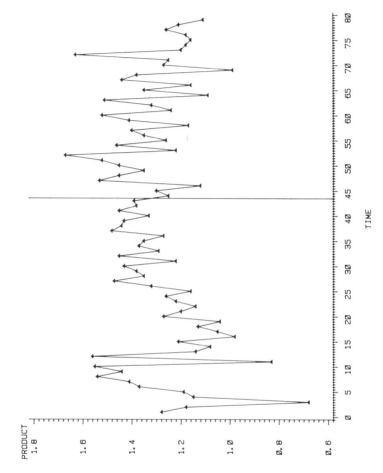

## Table 6-12
## Sites 12, 13, 14 and 15 Summary
### (Case 10)

| | Level | T-Stat | Lev Chg | T-Stat | Drift | T-Stat | Dft Chg | T-Stat |
|---|---|---|---|---|---|---|---|---|
| **Site 12** | | | | | | | | |
| Productivity (N=72, df=68) | 4.70 | 20.83 | -0.09 | -0.41 | 0.03 | 0.68 | -0.02 | -0.32 |
| Employment | 315.07 | 72.87 | 5.44 | 1.26 | -1.07 | -1.62 | -0.37 | -0.38 |
| Employment control (N=78, df=74) | 166.64 | 8.49 | 3.57 | 0.18 | 0.60 | 0.17 | -5.89 | -1.33 |
| Indirect/direct (N=78, df=74) | 0.65 | 47.56 | 0.00 | 0.10 | -0.00 | -0.27 | 0.00 | -0.68 |
| **Site 13** | | | | | | | | |
| Productivity (N=79, df=75) | 1.15 | 22.62 | 0.02 | 0.32 | 0.01 | 2.81 | -0.01 | -3.39+ |
| Employment | 97.02 | 57.77 | 3.42 | 2.12* | -0.03 | -0.03 | -0.63 | -0.56 |
| Employment control (N=40, df=36) | 18.77 | 36.39 | -0.46 | -1.00 | 0.08 | 0.70 | -0.10 | -0.85 |

| | | | | | | | | |
|---|---|---|---|---|---|---|---|---|
| **Site 14** | | | | | | | | |
| Productivity (N = 79, df = 75) | 3.49 | 12.32 | -0.39 | -1.11 | 0.01 | 1.13 | -0.02 | -0.88 |
| Employment | 22.65 | 19.25 | 0.80 | 0.77 | -0.27 | -1.06 | 0.21 | 0.79 |
| Employment control (N = 40, df = 36) | 18.77 | 36.39 | -0.46 | -1.00 | 0.08 | 0.70 | -0.10 | -0.85 |
| **Site 15** | | | | | | | | |
| Productivity (N = 79, df = 75) | 3.15 | 8.63 | -0.34 | -0.92 | 0.04 | 1.63 | -0.09 | -2.29* |
| Employment | 22.71 | 97.27 | -1.14 | -5.55 + | 0.21 | 4.31 | -0.22 | -4.32 + |
| Employment control (N = 40, df = 36) | 71.89 | 65.23 | 1.17 | 1.16 | 0.19 | 0.57 | -0.39 | -1.09 |

*p < .05, + p < .001

(t = -1.00, n.s.), remaining unchanged over time (t = -.85, n.s.).

Productivity at Site 15 was initially unchanged (t = -.92, n.s.). The trend, though, exhibited a statistically significant decrease (t = -2.29, p < .05). Employment suffered a statistically significant downturn in both the level and trend (t = -5.55 and t = -4.32, both p < .001). At the same time, industry employment showed an increase in level (t = 1.16, n.s.). Over time, industry employment experienced a downturn (t = -1.09, n.s.), though to a much lesser degree than that of the division.

This Improshare Plan did increase employee earnings. Site 12 paid a bonus 33 out of 35 months and Site 13 earned a bonus 27 of 35 months; Site 14 has paid a bonus less often, 14 of 34 months, but the bonuses have been much larger, for example, 5 have been in excess of 25 percent. The largest bonuses were paid at Site 15, where 12 of the 28 bonuses paid were more than 25 percent. Needless to say, the earning of differential bonuses, particularly when it had very little to do with indirect employee efforts, caused tension among the employees involved.

If the Improshare measure of productivity, that is, the bonus formula is examined, then productivity can be considered to have increased. There is no reason to assume that measure is a poor one and several managers interviewed indicated that Improshare provided the first real examination of productivity the sites had made. In comparison with Scanlon and Rucker measures, it comes closest to a pure output per hour ratio. *Yet, because of the quality of the measure of productivity at Sites 13-15, it is not possible to conclusively judge the effectiveness of Improshare.*

However, using the productivity data provided by the four sites, no immediate change in indirect labor productivity could be found. Moreover, at Sites 13 and 15, there was a negative trend over time. At Site 13, this can partially be explained by the introduction of new capital equipment following introduction of the Improshare Plan. This reduced the number of direct labor employees but increased the number of indirect workers required to maintain and service the new equipment.

One of the advantages of the Improshare Plan is that the bonus measurement system can be adapted for a large group of employees, yet need not apply to the entire employee complement as with the Rucker and Scanlon Plan. This was demonstrated in this case. However, there were several unintended consequences. First, there were differential earnings among groups of employees doing nearly the same work. Since it was unclear from the outset what impact indirect employees could have on productivity improvement, both workers and the management questioned the validity of the bonus formula. This problem was further compounded, as shown here, by the lack of good quality data to determine whether productivity had increased. In fact, no one ever knew whether productivity had increased, decreased, or remained the same. One of the most interesting overall findings from this study is that many companies are very poor at measuring their own productivity. This caused internal conflict within management as several of the divisions put forth proposals to modify the bonus formula. Needless to say, the union leadership also had internal difficulties in dealing with the differential earnings among the four groups of employees. The problem became further compounded when several employees working in one division were switched into another division for bonus calculation purposes only on the premise that their efforts primarily benefitted that division.

A strong argument can be made against the institution and structure of gainsharing at this site. The plan was for indirect employees only, whose efforts could not be clearly attached to company performance. There were four plans instead of one which would be typical. And there were no internal measures of productivity to evaluate the effectiveness of the gainsharing arrangement. This should not be considered a criticism of Improshare generally. Any form of gainsharing would have been inappropriate in this setting. In fact, Improshare is the only gainsharing approach that could have been even marginally appropriate in this situation. The counter argument to this criticism was put forth by a management proponent of the Plan. He took the position that since a commitment was made to raise the wages of the indirect workforce in negotiations, at the very least Improshare permitted the company to "get something for the money."

This position was not shared universally. The labor relations manager asserted a claim that was made at several other research sites as well. He argued that there was an over-reliance on the utilization of incentive systems (at this company, Halsey, Rowan and Improshare) to manage the workforce and facilitate production. Management, he alleged, relied on the incentive to manage employees, rather than supervision. Greater efforts should be made in the direction of improved supervisory management, meaningful employee involvement, and human resources programs to increase employee commitment and motivation.

## Conclusions

The ten cases presented serve to highlight the diversity in patterns of union-management cooperation and the variability of success. The stimulus for cooperation varied. In one instance (Case 1), cooperation (Scanlon Plan) occurred to save the plant, while in Case 8 (L-MC), it was to save large numbers of jobs. Differential outcomes occurred—the former was very successful and the latter a dismal failure.

In Cases 6, 7, and 10 cooperation centered around the introduction of new payment or incentive systems, while in three others—3, 4 (to win back concessions), and 5—the stimulus was for higher earnings. Thus the traditional union goal of higher earnings is very much present in these cooperative schemes. It is important to note that in Cases 6 and 7, very few bonuses were paid and "cooperation" ended. In Case 5, three Scanlon Plans of long duration paid large bonuses and this is an important element in their survival.

At least four cases represent situations in which jobs were immediately threatened (Cases 4, 8, and 9) or the plant was due to close. This is the greatest threat to the local union and its members, as well as to site management. Yet one has to question why situations are permitted to deteriorate to crisis proportions before adequate attention is paid to resolving the problems. Much of this can be explained by the adversary process of collective bargaining which has created a very high level of mistrust at the local level. If our industrial relations institutions are to be proactive rather than reactive, the level of mistrust must be reduced. Perhaps the current high level of cooperation will push parties in that direction.

In Cases 2 and 9, both plants which were part of the same multinational firm attempted to dramatically increase employee involvement. In Case 2, involvement was readily and overwhelmingly accepted, while in Case 9 involvement was resoundingly rejected by a vote of the employees. Case 3 presents a situation in which the impact of cooperation as measured by an improvement in quality and lower absenteeism was delayed by several months.

In this research, several measures of the impact of cooperation were utilized. They included organizational effectiveness measures (productivity, as defined by output per hour; level of employment; quality, absenteeism, turnover, tardiness, and grievances), program duration, and payment of bonuses. There are, however, other measures of effectiveness that could have been utilized as well. These include unit labor costs; the actual degree of employee involvement; employee attitudes toward work; employee mental health and safety; the impact of the cooperation on the internal affairs of the union and in its success in representing its members in collective bargaining; and the impact of cooperation on managerial decisionmaking and the quality of those decisions.

Finally, what characteristics separate the successful cases from the unsuccessful ones? Although the sample of firms was too small for a statistical determination of effectiveness, several factors were preliminarily identified. These included: type of ownership, technology, age composition of the workforce, program implementation strategies (i.e., training for supervisors and shop stewards), and the frequency of bonus payments. The cases presented in this chapter identify other additional factors.

In one case (8), the key management decisionmaker on site did not participate. In two others the failure of the key manager to involve himself in the cooperative process led to the demise of earlier efforts (4 and 9). In two cases (2 and 5), there was a strong desire by management for employee participation, while in another a structure was put in place for participation but very little shop floor decisionmaking was permitted (Case 7). Managerial problems unrelated to the unionized workforce were present and overcome in one case (4), but continued to be a source of frustration in another (Case 8). Hence, the attitudes, values, and competence of the management have a great deal to do with the success of the cooperative effort.

Where expertise is required to assist the parties, particularly in devising bonus formulas, most firms utilized widely known and respected consultants. Along the same lines, one Labor-Management Committee (Case 4) was assisted by the staff of an Area Committee and was very successful, while another (Case 8) had no similar support and proved to be very unsuccessful.

Questionable practices were associated with the calculation of bonuses in two cases (6 and 7). The lack of bonus earnings combined with the impression of manipulation led to termination of the cooperative effort. Few bonuses were paid in spite of the fact that there was evidence to suggest that productivity had increased.

Several successful cases (1, 2, 3, 4, and 5) paid high to moderate bonuses, at times equalling as much as 25 percent of pay. Yet, most of these firms experienced and survived extended periods of very limited or no bonuses. Thus payment of a bonus is not by itself a sole condition for success. For example, in Case 10, large and frequent bonuses were consistently paid, yet there remains some doubt whether such a bonus record was justified by the productivity experience in this instance.

## NOTES

1. Originally there were five categories. Very Positive or Very Negative Impact was indicated when the t-statistic measuring the impact of the change was significant at the $p < .05$, $p < .01$, or $p < .001$ levels. A Positive or Negative Impact was indicated by a t-statistics of $\pm 1.00$, while t-statistics of less than $\pm .99$ were classified as no change. The rationale for doing this stemmed from the small size of the sample, the fact that the number of observations in each time-series was roughly equivalent, the conservative nature of the time-series test, and the desire for preliminary identification of some of the determinants of success.

2. Note that a "Positive Impact" on absenteeism, turnover, tardiness, grievances occurred when there was a decrease in rate.

3. Several of the cases discussed in this section are also presented in a recently published paper: M. Schuster, "The Impact of Union-Management Cooperation on Productivity and Employment." *Industrial and Labor Relations Review,* 1983, Vol. 36(3), 415-430.

4. The productivity data could not be statistically analyzed due to the manner in which they were provided. Instead, they were examined graphically.

5. *Supplemental Agreement,* p. 30.

6. Ibid., p. 30.

7. All quotations are from the minutes of the meetings of the Union-Management Study Group on Productivity and Quality of Worklife. No further referencing is provided.

8. Shop floor employees are often classified as direct and indirect employees. Direct employees are those who work on the machinery, for example, lathe operators. Indirect employees provide a support function, for example, material handling or stores.

9. This is the same as added value, that is sales value minus cost of goods sold.

# Chapter 7

# Conclusions


This chapter presents some of the major findings of the research, along with the policy implications from these findings. There are five sections in this chapter. Three correspond to chapters 4, 5, and 6, that is, they address the structure, process, and impact of union-management cooperation. The final two segments identify and discuss the methodological findings and discuss future research issues.

## The Structure of Cooperation

There were six types of interventions investigated for this research. These included three types of gainsharing plans—Scanlon, Rucker, and Improshare Plans—as well as Quality Circles, Labor-Management Committees, and Quality of Worklife projects. The results of this analysis are reported in detail in chapter 4. Several important findings are noted below.

*The six interventions vary significantly in their underlying philosophy.* Scanlon Plans and Quality Circles are based upon a more humanistic view of workplace management, in contrast to Improshare Plans, which are primarily group incentive programs. Rucker Plans are also more directly based on economic incentives, but do provide for some limited employee participation.

*None of these interventions is a substitute for competent management, good union-management relations, or*

217

*responsible union leadership.* Organizations without these ingredients may not be adequately prepared for an extensive organizational change. In these instances, Labor-Management Committees are particularly effective at changing the industrial relations environment, thereby permitting more significant interventions, for example, Quality Circles, gainsharing or Quality of Worklife projects, to be instituted.

*If the management of a company is not fully committed to employee participation, then implementing involvement structures (for example, Quality Circles) will not lead to improved organizational effectiveness.* Employee involvement requires that management be willing to relinquish some control over workplace behavior. Employees have to be trusted to act responsibly and managers must be willing to listen to employee ideas.

*Supervisors play a key role in improving workplace performance.* Unfortunately, the quality of American production supervision appears to be mediocre, at best. This problem is further compounded by the lack of resources firms expend for supervisory training.

*The bonus formulas are an excellent means of equitably sharing organizational improvements.* However, they must be developed with great care and caution since they are difficult to change once implemented. Consultants serve a useful role in developing the formulas. There is one caveat. In a workplace environment of great distrust, and particularly when no bonus is received, the calculation of the bonus each month can be a source of additional animosity, as workers question the integrity of the formula and the honesty of management in assembling the figures.

## The Process of Cooperation

Analysis of the process of cooperation considered the means by which the parties changed their relationship. These findings are reported in detail in chapter 5. Several general conclusions were drawn.

*There were a number of reasons for companies and unions to enter into a cooperative relationship.* These include a desire to increase productivity, improve labor-management relations, increase wages, and institute a new incentive program. In many instances, the initial stimuli influenced the choice of intervention. Thus, gainsharing programs are likely to be more successful at improving productivity than Labor-Management Committees. However, L-MCs will likely be a more effective strategy for preparing an organization for in-depth change. Additionally, where the stimulus for a cooperative effort includes both improvement of productivity and improved labor-management relations, a program such as the Scanlon Plan can offer a beneficial result even where the organization experiences no significant increase in productivity.

*There will be no cooperation if the traditional collective bargaining process is effective at resolving organizational difficulties.* Companies and unions still prefer to interact with one another as they have since the inception of collective bargaining. At this time, there is very little evidence (the popular press notwithstanding) to suggest that a new era of union-management relations based upon trust and cooperation is on the horizon. Indeed, companies and unions will continue to approach industrial relations pragmatically and will cooperate only when it is in their interest to do so.

*The cooperative process requires neutrals and consulting expertise.* The parties need the expertise of outsiders to assist them in formulating and implementing cooperative programs. For example, in this research, Labor-Management Committees were far more effective when they were guided by the expertise of the staff of Area Labor-Management Committees. Expansion of the number of Area L-MCs and increasing their resources would be very useful and should result in increased union-management cooperation and more effective Labor-Management Committees.

*There has been an increasing interest in employee participation at the workplace.* Although many companies and unions are attempting to provide employees with an opportunity to influence decisionmaking, there is as yet no concrete evidence as to the actual quantity and quality of that participation, nor what effect it has on organizational effectiveness.

*There is still no indication that guarantees of employment security will become commonplace in American industrial relations.* Nearly all firms studied appear to be unwilling or unable to guarantee workers a job.

*Unions have less confidence in the cooperative process than management, which tends to believe it will be likely to produce desired organizational results.* In addition, management also believes that, in practice, there are more benefits to be gained through cooperation.

## The Impact of Cooperation

There were ten measures of program impact. These were level and drift changes in productivity, quality, employment, turnover, absenteeism, tardiness, grievances, plus data on program survival after two and five years, frequency of bonus earnings, and rater effectiveness. There were many important results, several of which are highlighted below.

*Union-management cooperation can lead to significant improvements in productivity.* Of 23 sites, productivity improved in 11 and was unchanged in 10. Thus, it appears that companies and unions have very little to risk and much to gain from a cooperative venture. In 16 of 23 firms bonuses were paid to employees more than 50 percent of the time. This indicates that unions can supplement wage gains from collective bargaining through union-management cooperation and gainsharing.

*Employment tends to be more influenced by general industry conditions than by any other factor.* Thus, employment at firms with cooperative programs frequently tends

to follow the industry trend. However, there were instances where industry employment dropped and the site
remained stable. Several companies claimed that the
cooperative effort had helped them to be more cost competitive. This permitted the plants to acquire a greater
share of the available business, thereby helping to stabilize
employment.

*Labor-management relations can be significantly improv-
ed through union-management cooperation.* In the vast
majority of cases, union-management relations were improved. Greater trust and confidence were established,
and more frequent and substantive problemsolving interaction occurred. In many cases, both union and
management respondents reported that a new perspective
on their relationship had developed.

*Data are still too preliminary to determine the factors
which influence success and failure in cooperative ventures.* However, there is some support for the factors
outlined in chapter 2 (employment security, employee
involvement, plantwide compensation distributed on a
monthly basis, an effective acceptance strategy, and
technology) as well as others that were identified in the
case analysis presented in chapter 5. Further research is required in order to create a sufficiently large sample to conduct such an analysis.

## Methodological Findings

Previous research on union-management cooperation has
been severely criticized on methodological grounds. One of
the major goals of this study was to further develop and
refine strategies for studying cooperation and change in
unionized settings. These observations are the result of the
field work conducted during this study and ongoing
monitoring of the cooperative union-management and quality of worklife literature.

*A program evaluation approach can be utilized to study
cooperative union-management strategies.* Union-

management cooperation can be studied in the same manner as other interventions. Thus the strategies, techniques, and procedures utilized by evaluation researchers become appropriate. Industrial relations researchers can adapt the rich body of evaluation literature to study interventions such as labor-management committees, quality of worklife programs, and gainsharing. Well-designed case studies are likely to provide the best method for studying cooperative programs.

*Evaluations of cooperation and change should be longitudinal and include performance measures of effectiveness both before and after the introduction of the program.* Studies conducted over short time frames do not address the process and impact of change when the newness and excitement of the "experiment" have worn. There has been too much research emphasis on attitudes toward cooperation and descriptive studies of the cooperative process and only a small number of studies have examined the "before and after" effects of cooperation. Thus, what is needed are studies conducted over an extended time frame, using measures such as output per hour, scrap rates, unexcused absences, etc., with pre- and post-change data being analyzed.

*There is a need to study unsuccessful cases.* There are very few studies of failure in union-management cooperation. Yet, there is general agreement that many experiments fail. Little is known of the dynamics that result in failure. Much could be learned and transmitted to other bargaining relationships from the study of unsuccessful cases. Unfortunately, unsuccessful cases are generally more difficult to locate and it is often difficult to get the participants to discuss their experiences.

*It is very difficult to get company and union representatives to participate in field studies of the cooperative process.* There is a fear that the introduction of a researcher will have a destabilizing infuence on the cooperative process.

## Future Research Issues

An outcome of this research has been to identify seven areas for further investigation. The seven are:

(1) Investigation of additional research sites;
(2) Continued analysis of selected sites, including sites where cooperation has ended;
(3) Study of additional forms of union-management cooperation;
(4) Study of worker-management cooperation in non-union firms;
(5) Addition of attitudinal variables;
(6) Analysis of the calculation of the bonus formulas used in gainsharing plans;
(7) Improving the research design and analytical techniques over previous research.

### Investigation of Additional Research Sites

There is a need to continue to build the size of the sample of interventions. The current sample of 38 remains too small to permit an in-depth evaluation of the determinants of success and failure. Increasing the sample size would permit cross-sectional analysis of variables such as employee composition, type of interventions, employee participation, technology, and size, frequency and amount of bonus payments.

### Continued Analysis of Selected Sites Including Those Where Cooperation has Ended

The initial post-intervention time frame of two to three years of analysis should be expanded to at least five. In this way it will be possible to determine whether the impact was long term rather than temporary, and whether cooperation has survived some natural occurrences, for example, negotiation of a new contract, union elections, change of plant management, and economic downturn.

Additionally, cooperation at several sites has ended. It would be very interesting, and important, to study the performance of the firm and union-management relations during the post-cooperation period.

### Study of Additional Forms of Union-Management Cooperation

There has been a significant increase in the use of Quality Circles. The Circles have become pervasive not only in the private sector, but also in hospitals and the public sector. Very little evaluation research of the impact of these programs has occurred.

Another form of cooperation where research has been limited has been profit-sharing plans. The popular press has reported an increase in profit-sharing plans. These plans closely resemble gainsharing except that they utilize a global measure of organizational performance rather than productivity. A methodology similar to the one used in this research would be appropriate for assessing the impact of Quality Circles and profit sharing.

### Study of Worker-Management Cooperation in Nonunion Firms

Although not a major direction of the research, five nonunion firms with cooperative experiments similar to those in unionized firms participated in this research. Further investigation of these plans would make it possible to draw some conclusions about the differences and similarities between union and nonunion firms.

### Addition of Attitudinal Variables

It is important to determine which attitudinal constructs best explain employee motivation to improve productivity and increase effectiveness in the cooperative endeavors. Expectancy, equity, and commitment models have been offered as possibilities. However, data to substantiate any construct do not exist at this time. This area should be given priority consideration in future research.

## Analysis of the Calculation of Bonus Formulas in Gainsharing Plans

One common question frequently posed by management and union respondents dealt with the bonus formula measurement. In essence, many respondents wanted to know what the results would have been if another bonus formula had been utilized. In this research there was one site with a Rucker Plan which provided sufficient data to simulate the Scanlon Plan bonus formula. Wide differences in payouts occurred. At the present time this evidence is preliminary and further investigation at more sites is needed.

## Improving the Research Design and Analytical Techniques

One goal of this research was to develop the methodological techniques to scientifically evaluate experiments in productivity improvements and union-management cooperation. The extensive findings from this aspect of the study are presented in chapter 3. In particular, better software packages for time-series impact assessment have recently become available. Also, extending the length of the time-series would enable investigators to better fit time-series (ARIMA) statistical models.

# REFERENCES

Ahern, R.W. *Positive Labor Relations: Plant Labor Management Committees and the Collective Bargaining Process.* Report prepared for the Buffalo-Erie County Labor-Management Council, April 1978.

Ahern, R.W. *The Area-Wide Labor-Management Committee: The Buffalo Experience.* Report prepared for the Buffalo-Erie County Labor-Management Council, November 1979.

Beaumont, P.B. & Deaton, D.R. "Organizational Development and Change in a Union-Management Context: The Voluntary Establishment of Joint Health and Safety Committees in Britian." *Organization Studies,* 1981, 2(4), 331-345.

Bower, C.P., Podia, W.L. & Glass, G.V. *TMS: Two Fortran IV Programs for Analysis of Time-Series Experiments.* Boulder: Laboratory of Educational Research, University of Colorado, 1974.

Box, G.E.P. & Jenkins, G.M. *Time-Series Analysis: Forecasting and Control.* San Francisco: Holden Day, 1970.

Brooks, H.E. "The Armour Automation Committee Experience." *Proceedings of the 21st Annual Winter Meeting of the Industrial Relations Research Association,* 1968, 137-143.

Bureau of National Affairs. *Basic Patterns in Union Contracts.* Washington, DC: BNA, 1970, 1975, 1979.

Bushe, G.R. *Exploring Managerial Resistance to Worker Problem-Solving Groups: Some Comparative Data.* Paper presented at the Annual Meeting of the Academy of Management, 1983.

*Business Week.* "The New Industrial Relations," May 11, 1981, 84-99.

Campbell, D.T. "Degrees of Freedom" and the case study. In T.D. Cook and C.S. Reichardt, eds., *Qualitative and Quantitative Methods in Evaluation Research.* Beverly Hills: Sage Publications, 1979.

Campbell, D.T. & Stanley, J.C. *Experimental and Quasi-Experimental Designs for Research.* Chicago: Rand McNally, 1963.

Chamberlain, N.W. & Kuhn, J.W. *Collective Bargaining* (2nd ed.). New York: McGraw Hill, 1965.

"Concessionary Bargaining: Will the New Cooperation Last?" *Business Week,* June 14, 1982.

Cook, T. & Campbell, D. "The Design and Conduct of Quasi-Experiments and True Experiments in Field Settings." In M. Dunnette, ed., *Handbook of Industrial and Organizational Psychology.* Chicago: Rand McNally, 1976.

Cook, T.D. & Campbell, D.T. *Quasi-Experimentation: Design and Analysis Issues for Field Settings.* Chicago: Rand McNally, 1979.

Cook, T.D. & Reichardt, C.S. *Qualitative and Quantitative Methods in Evaluation Research.* Beverly Hills: Sage, 1979.

Corbett, L.P. "The Health Care Experience." *Proceedings of the 39th Annual Winter Meeting of the Industrial Relations Research Association,* 1982, 152-158.

Cummings, T.G. & Molloy, E.S. *Improving Productivity and the Quality of Work Life.* New York: Praeger, 1977.

Dale, E. "Increasing Productivity Through Labor-Management Cooperation." *Industrial and Labor Relations Review,* 1949, 2, 33-44.

Davenport, R. "Enterprise for Every Man." *Fortune,* January 1950, 41(1), 51-58.

Derber, M. & Flanigan, K. *A Survey of Joint Labor-Management Cooperation Committees in Unionized Private Enterprises in the State of Illinois, 1979.* Washington, DC: U.S. Department of Labor, 1980.

Dewar, D.L. *The Quality Circle Guide to Participative Management.* Englewood Cliffs, N.J.: Prentice Hall, 1980.

Drexler, J.A. & Lawler, E.E. "A Union-Management Cooperation Project to Improve the Quality of Work Life." *Journal of Applied Behavioral Science,* 1977, 13, 373-387.

Driscoll, J.W. *A Multiple-Constituency, Control Group Evaluation of the Scanlon Plan.* Paper presented at the Annual Meeting of the Academy of Management, 1982.

Driscoll, J.W. "Labor-Management Panels: Three Case Studies." *Monthly Labor Review,* 1980, 103(6), 41-44.

Dubin, R. "Union-Management Co-operation and Productivity." *Industrial and Labor Relations Review,* 1949, 2, 195-209.

Dunlop, J.T. *Industrial Relations Systems.* New York: Holt, 1958.

Dyer, L., Lipsky, D.B. & Kochan, T.A. "Union Attitudes Toward Management Cooperation." *Industrial Relations,* 1977, 16(2) 163-172.

Fein, M. *Improshare: An Alternative to Traditional Managing.* Norcross, GA: Institute of Industrial Engineers, 1981.

Fein, M. "Improving Productivity by Improved Productivity Sharing." *The Conference Board Record,* 1976, 13(7), 44-49.

French, W. *The Personnel Management Process* (4th ed.). Boston: Houghton Mifflin, 1978.

Frost, C. "The Scanlon Plan: Anyone for Free Enterprise?" *MSU Business Topics,* 1978, 26(1), 25-33.

Frost, C.F., Wakeley, J.H. & Ruh, R.A. *The Scanlon Plan for Organization Development: Identity, Participation, and Equity.* East Lansing, MI: Michigan State University Press, 1974.

Fukami, C.V. & Larson, E. *The Relationship Between Union Commitment and Organizational Commitment: Dual Loyalty Reexamined.* Paper presented at the Annual Meeting of the Academy of Management, August 1982.

Gilson, T. & Lefcowitz, M. "A Plant Wide Productivity Bonus in a Small Factory: Study of an Unsuccessful Case." *Industrial and Labor Relations Review,* 1957, 10(2), 284-296.

Glass, G.V., Willson, V.L. & Gottman, J.M. *Design and Analysis of Time Series Experiments.* Boulder, CO: Colorado Associated University Press, 1975.

Goodman, P.S. *Assessing Organizational Change: The Rushton Quality of Work Experiment.* New York: Wiley, 1979.

Goodman, P.S. "The Scanlon Plan: A Need for Conceptual and Empirical Models." Paper presented to the American Psychological Association, September 1973.

Gray, D.A., Sinicropi, A.V. & Hughes, P.A. "From Conflict to Cooperation: A Joint Union-Management Goal Setting and Problem-Solving Program." *Proceedings of the 34th Annual Winter Meeting of the Industrial Relations Research Association,* 1982, 26-32.

Greenberg, L. *A Practical Guide to Productivity Measurement.* Washington, DC: Bureau of National Affairs, 1973.

Healy, J.J., ed. *Creative Collective Bargaining.* Englewood Cliffs, NJ: Prentice Hall, 1965.

Helfgott, R. *Group Wage Incentives: Experience with the Scanlon Plan.* New York: Industrial Relations Counsellors, Memo #141, 1962.

Heneman, H., Jr. "Research Roundup: Worker Participation and Productivity." *The Personnel Administrator,* April 1979, 65-78.

Horvitz, W.L. "The ILWU-PMA Mechanization and Modernization Agreement." *Proceedings of the 21st Annual Meeting of the Industrial Relations Research Association,* 1968, 144-151.

230

Jick, Todd D. "Mixing Qualitative and Quantitative Methods: Triangulation in Action." *Administrative Science Quarterly,* 1979, 4, 602-611.

Katz, D. & Kahn, R.L. *The Social Psychology of Organizations.* New York: Wiley, 1966.

Katzell, R.A. & Yankelovich, D. *Work, Productivity, and Job Satisfaction.* New York: Harcourt, 1975.

Kochan, T.A. *Labor Management Relations Research Priorities for the 1980's: Final Report to the Secretary of Labor.* Washington, DC: U.S. Department of Labor, 1980.

Kochan, T.A. & Dyer, L. "A Model of Organizational Change in the Context of Union-Management Relations." *Journal of Applied Behavioral Science.* 1976, 12(2) 59-78.

Kochan, T.A., Lipsky, D.B. & Dyer, L. "Collective Bargaining and the Quality of Work: The Views of Local Union Activists." *Proceedings of the 27th Annual Winter Meeting of the Industrial Relations Research Association,* 1974, 150-162.

Kochan, T.A., Dyer, L. & Lipsky, D.B. *The Effectiveness of Union-Management Safety and Health Committees.* Kalamazoo, MI: W.E. Upjohn Institute, 1977.

Lawler, E.E., III & Drexler, J.A. "Dynamics of Establishing Cooperative Quality of Work Life Projects." *Monthly Labor Review,* 1978, 101(3), 23-28.

Leone, R.D., Eleey, M.F., Watkins, D.W., Gershenfeld, J.E. *The Origins, Structure, and Operation of Areawide Labor-Management Committees.* A report submitted to the Labor-Management Services Administration, United States Department of Labor, 1981.

Lesieur, F.G. "Local Union Experiences with a Cooperation Plan." *Proceedings of the 4th Annual Meeting of the Industrial Relations Research Association,* 1951, 174-181.

Lesieur, F.G., ed. *The Scanlon Plan: A Frontier in Labor-Management Cooperation.* Cambridge, MA: The MIT Press, 1958.

Lesieur, F.G. & Puckett, E.S. "The Scanlon Plan: Past, Present, and Future." *Proceedings of the 21st Annual Winter Meeting of the Industrial Relations Research Association,* 1968, 71-80.

Luthans, F. & Kreitner, R. *Organizational Behavior Modification.* Glenview, IL: Scott, Foresman, 1975.

Macy, B.A. "The Bolivar Quality of Work Life Program: A Longitudinal Behavioral and Performance Assessment." *Proceedings of the 32nd Annual Winter Meeting of the Industrial Relations Research Association,* 1979, 83-93.

Macy, B.A. & Mirvis, P.H. "A Methodology for Assessment of Quality of Work Life and Organizational Effectiveness in Behavioral Economic Terms." *Administrative Science Quarterly,* 1976, 21(2), 212-226.

Maye, W.T. "Presidential Labor-Management Committees: Productive Failures." *Industrial and Labor Relations Review,* 1980, 34(1), 51-66.

Mayer, L. *Establishing In-Plant Committees: An Introduction to a Data-Based Model.* A paper presented at the Symposium on Area Labor-Management Committees, July 21-25, 1980.

Mccain, L.J. & McCleary, R. "The Statistical Analysis of the Simple Interrupted Time-Series and Quasi-Experiment." In T.D. Cook & D.T. Campbell, eds., *Quasi-Experimentation: Design and Analysis Issues for Field Settings.* Chicago: Rand McNally, 1979.

McGregor, D. *The Human Side of Enterprise.* New York: McGraw Hill, 1960.

Metzger, B.L., ed. *Increasing Productivity Through Profit Sharing.* Evanston, IL: Profit Sharing Research Foundation, 1981.

Metzger, B.L. *Profit Sharing in Seventy-Eight Longitudinal Comparisons.* Evanston, IL: Profit Sharing Research Foundation, 1975.

Mohrman, S.A. *The Impact of Quality Circles: A Conceptual View.* A paper presented at the conference on Current Directions in Productivity—Evolving Japanese and American Practices, Houston, May 13, 1982.

Moore, B.E. *A Plant-Wide Productivity Plan in Action.* A report for the National Center for Productivity and Quality of Working Life, 1975.

Moore, B.E. & Goodman, P.S. *Factors Affecting the Impact of a Company-Wide Incentive Program on Productivity.* A final report submitted to the National Commission on Productivity, January 1973.

Moore, B.E. & Ross, T.L. *The Scanlon Way to Improved Productivity: A Practical Guide.* New York: Wiley, 1978.

Nadler, D.A., Hanlon, M. & Lawler, E.E., III. "Factors Influencing the Success of Labor-Management Quality of Work Life Projects." *Journal of Occupational Behavior,* 1980, 1(1), 53-67.

National Center for Productivity and Quality of Working Life. *Directory of Labor-Management Committees,* 1977 & 1978.

National Center for Productivity and Quality of Working Life. *Establishing a Communitywide Labor-Management Committee.* Washington, DC: U.S. Government Printing Office, 1978(b).

232

National Center for Productivity and Quality of Working Life. *Improving Governmental Productivity: Selected Case Studies.* Washington, DC: U.S. Government Printing Office, 1977.

National Center for Productivity and Quality of Working Life. *Improving Productivity.* Washington, DC: U.S. Government Printing Office, 1976.

National Center for Productivity and Quality of Working Life. *Labor-Management Committees in the Public Sector: Experiences of Eight Committees.* Washington, DC: U.S. Government Printing Office, 1975.

National Center for Productivity and Quality of Working Life. *Productivity and Job Security: Attrition—Benefits and Problems.* Washington, DC: U.S. Government Printing Office, 1977.

National Center for Productivity and Quality of Working Life. *Productivity and Job Security: Retraining to Adapt to Technological Change.* Washington, DC: U.S. Government Printing Office, 1977.

National Center for Productivity and Quality of Working Life. *Recent Initiatives in Labor-Management Cooperation,* Washington, DC: U.S. Government Printing Office, 1978.

New York Stock Exchange Office of Economic Research. *People and Productivity: A Challenge to Corporate America,* 1982.

Pack, D.J. *A Computer Program for the Analysis of Time Series Models Using the Box-Jenkins Philosophy.* Hatboro, PA: Automatic Forecasting Systems (1977).

Perlman, S. *A Theory of the Labor Movement.* New York: Augustus Kelley, 1949.

Peterson, R.B. & Tracy, L. "Testing a Behavioral Theory Model of Labor Negotiations." *Industrial Relations,* 1977, 16, 35-50.

Petersen, S.A., Leitko, T.A. & Miles, W.G. "Worker Participation and the Spillover Effect: The Case of Labor-Management Committees." *Economic and Industrial Democracy,* 1981, 2, 27-44.

Ponak, A.M. & Fraser, C.R.P. "Union Activists' Support for Joint Programs." *Industrial Relations,* 1979, 18(2), 197-209.

Popular, J.J. *Perspective: Area Labor-Management Committees.* A paper presented at the Symposium on Area Labor-Management Committees, Cornell University, July 21-25, 1980.

Poulin, G.J. "Three Survival Issues." Remarks to the International Association of Machinists and Aerospace Workers Western States Conference, July 15, 1982.

233

Puckett, E.S. "Productivity Achievements: A Measure of Success." In F.G. Lesieur, ed., *The Scanlon Plan: A Frontier in Labor-Management Cooperation.* Cambridge, MA: The MIT Press, 1958.

Purcell, T. *The Worker Speaks His Mind on Company and Union.* Cambridge, MA: Harvard University Press, 1954.

Ray, P.E. "The Retail Food Industry." *Proceedings of the 34th Annual Winter Meeting of the Industrial Relations Research Association,* 1982, 145-151.

Rosenberg, R.D. & Rosenstein, E. "Participation and Productivity: An Empirical Study." *Industrial and Labor Relations Review,* April 1980, 33(3).

Rosenthal, R. *Experimenter Effects in Behavioral Research.* New York: Appleton-Century-Crofts, 1966.

Roy, D. "Quota Restriction and Goldbricking in a Machine Shop. *American Journal of Sociology* 1952, 57(5), 427-552.

Ruh, R.A., Wallace, R.L. & Frost, C.F. "Management Attitudes and the Scanlon Plan." *Industrial Relations,* 1973, 12, 282-288.

Schlesinger, L.A. *Quality of Work Life and the Supervisor.* New York: Praeger, 1982.

Schuster, M. "Conceptual and Empirical Issues in Union-Management Cooperation Research." Paper presented at the Annual Meeting of the Academy of Management, 1982.

Schuster, M. "Forty Years of Scanlon Plan Research: A Review of the Descriptive and Empirical Literature." *International Yearbook of Organizational Democracy, 1,* 1983a, 53-71.

Schuster, M. *Labor-Management Productivity Programs: Their Operation and Effect on Employment and Productivity.* A final report to the United States Department of Labor, Employment and Training Administration, 1980. Available through the National Technical Information Service.

Schuster, M. "Research Model of Labor-Management Productivity Program Effectiveness. *Academy of Management Proceedings,* 1979, 246-250.

Schuster, M. "The Scanlon Plan: A Longitudinal Analysis," *Journal of Applied Behavioral Science,* 20(1), 1984, 23-38.

Schuster, M. "The Impact of Union-Management Cooperation on Productivity and Employment." *Industrial and Labor Relations Review,* 1983b, 36(3), 415-430.

234

Shiron, A. *Industrial Cooperation and Adjustment to Technological Change: A Study of Joint Management Union Committees.* Madison, Wisconsin, Ph.D. thesis, 1968.

Shultz, G.P. "Worker Participation on Production Problems: A Discussion of Experience with the 'Scanlon Plan.'" *Personnel,* 1951, 28(3), 201-211.

Siegel, I.H. & Weinberg, E. *Labor-Management Cooperation: The American Experience.* Kalamazoo, MI: W.E. Upjohn Institute for Employment Research, 1982.

Slichter, S.H., Healy, J.J. & Livernash, E.R. *The Impact of Collective Bargaining on Management.* Washington, DC: The Brookings Institution, 1960.

Stagner, R. "Dual Allegiance as a Problem in Modern Society." *Personnel Psychology,* 1954, 1, 41-47.

Steers, R.M. "Antecedents and Outcomes of Organizational Commitment." *Administrative Science Quarterly,* 1977, 22(1), 45-56.

Steers, R.M. & Porter, L.W. *Motivation and Work Behavior.* New York: McGraw-Hill, 1979.

Tait, R. "Some Experiences with a Union-Management Cooperation Plan." *Proceedings of the 4th Annual Meeting of the Industrial Relations Research Association,* 1952, 167-237.

Thrasher, B. "Productivity and Employment Security." *The Conference Board Record,* 1976, 13(7), 42-43.

United States Department of Commerce, Bureau of the Census. *1980 United States Census of Population, Volume 1.* Washington, DC: U.S. Government Printing Office, 1982.

United States Department of Labor, Bureau of Labor Statistics. *BLS Handbook of Methods* (Bulletin 1910). Washington, DC: U.S. Government Printing Office, 1976.

United States Department of Labor, Bureau of Labor Statistics. *Employment and Earnings, United States, 1909-78* (Bulletin 1312-11). Washington, DC: U.S. Government Printing Office, 1979.

United States Department of Labor, Bureau of Labor Statistics. *Major Collective Bargaining Agreements: Layoff, Recall and Work Sharing Procedures* (Bulletin 1425-13). Washington, DC: U.S. Government Printing Office, 1971.

United States Department of Labor, Labor-Management Services Administration. *Resource Guide to Labor-Management Cooperation.* Washington, DC: U.S. Government Printing Office, 1982.

235

United States General Accounting Office. *Department of Labor has Failed to Take the Lead in Promoting Private Sector Productivity.* Gaithersburg, MD: GAO, 1980a.

United States General Accounting Office. *Productivity Sharing Programs: Can They Contribute to Productivity Improvement?* Gaithersburg, MD: GAO, 1981.

United States General Accounting Office. *The Council on Wage and Price Stability has not Stressed Productivity in its Efforts to Reduce Inflation.* Gaithersburg, MD: GAO, 1980b.

Walton, R.E. & McKersie, R.B. *A Behavioral Theory of Labor Negotiations.* New York: McGraw-Hill, 1965.

Walton, R.E. & Schlesinger, L.A. "Do Supervisors Thrive in Parcipative Work Systems?" *Organizational Dynamics,* Winter 1979, 25-38.

Watts, G.E. "Quality of Work Life." Remarks to the National Labor-Management Conference, Washington, DC, September 9-10, 1982.

Webb, E.J., Campbell, D.T., Schwartz, R.D., Sechrest, L. & Grove, J.B. *Nonreactive Measures in the Social Sciences.* Boston: Houghton-Mifflin Co., 1981.

White, J.K. "The Scanlon Plan: Causes and Correlates of Success." *Academy of Management Journal.* 1979, 22(2), 292-312.

Woodward, J. *Industrial Organization: Theory and Practice.* London: Oxford University Press, 1965.